Basic
gardening

Everything you need to make your garden grow

S. Engels, V. Goldstück, M. Görlach, R. Simoni

Basic gardening
Contents

Basic gardening is fun

Few basic things in life are really fun and make us happy, but gardening is definitely one of them. What's the reason?

Because it's pure pleasure! Because it has to do with fantasy, discovery, and adventure. When you can have red poppies, purple lavender, and fresh wild strawberries straight from the balcony and zucchini in a flowerpot, you get a real sense of achievement. These are all simple pleasures, but they are sure to make you happy.

How can we achieve this heavenly state and how long will it take?

That's what we asked ourselves, too, when we started gardening. After all, gardening is very much a matter of experience and know-how. Surely you can get it all wrong. You can't get started just like that, just because you feel like it. Or can you?

That thought made us realize that something was missing. And that realization gave us a push in the right direction: a book to make the first, faltering steps to a gardening paradise easy and enjoyable. A book that doesn't take itself too seriously. Why does gardening always have to be so serious? We would have loved to have that sort of book when we first started gardening, and because we couldn't find one, we have written one.

And here it is. *Basic Gardening* is about trying things out and letting your imagination run free, with over 150 favorite plants and I-can-do-that-too ideas for city gardeners, balcony owners, and other unconventional gardeners. It contains all the basics you need to get started quickly and easily with lots of fun and no stress. There are uncomplicated, amusing, romantic, and labor-saving ideas for balconies, windows, yards, and gardens. It's really easy to acquire a green thumb. Basic gardening is fun!

Know-How

Getting started

"I love that one!"

"Then get it. What is it?"

"Looks like a gigantic poppy. That would do for my balcony... but would it grow well there?"

"Look at the plastic label. Perhaps that says what it is."

"It says *Papaver orientale* 'Perry's White.' Great! That doesn't tell me anything. What should I do?"

"You've got two options. You can go home, read up on it, and maybe save this particular Perry's life. It's a bit of a bummer, though, to leave without the poppy. On the other hand, you'll have learned something."

"Hmm. And the other option?"

"Buy it on impulse and get it wrong. Down-side — the poppy might not make it. Upside — you'll have learned something by experimenting."

"If that's the choice, then I'll take the poppy with me."

Both methods are perfectly okay. But what about planning? Yes, but like all things in life, every-thing in moderation. What you need to know is the Basic stuff. And that's just what we're going to show you now.

Savvy shopping

"What kinds of plants are there — apart from those you get as a present or buy at the supermarket? And where would you find them anyway?"

It's fun buying plants! Once you go plant shopping, you'll want to do it over and over, because there are endless varieties to enjoy and you always get new ideas. You can buy plants in so many places — at yard and garage sales and at swap meets, at farmers' markets, from nurseries, in hardware stores, at florists, in gift stores, and at your local supermarket.

A whole world in the wild

The widest selection is found at big garden centers. They are almost a whole world in themselves. There is absolutely EVERYTHING here: delicate summer flowers and robust fruit trees, lawnmowers, garden gnomes with mobile phones, gardening gloves, Mason jars — not forgetting the ornament section! Here you can find more pots than you can imagine. Fancy gold pots, stylish metal buckets, laughing plastic pumpkins, rustic terra-cotta, amphoras with antique trim — you'll need hours to see them all, you'll have a thousand new ideas (mini-pond with water lilies, bamboo pergola), you won't be able to decide, and you'll be loading up the car with something completely different from what you had in mind. But you'll still think it's fantastic.

And where else?

Specialist nurseries sometimes stock plants you won't find in the large garden centers, such as unusual herbs. They are also often less expensive. And a trip to a small, often family-run nursery is fun. Finding favorite nurseries can become a hobby! Street markets or farmers' markets are another—often inexpensive—source of plants. This is a good place to look for herbs and vegetables, such as early beans.

You can also order from the catalogues of major suppliers and other mail order companies who specialize in seeds, for instance, or exotic plants, shrubs, or roses. Risky? Not at all, it works without a hitch. The mail order nurseries send your plants packed in special boxes with plastic protection. Some only ship in spring and fall, not in the hot summer months, to ensure that the plants arrive in good condition. (Resources, page 138)

Take a good look

Wherever you buy, always choose plants that look really healthy. If the soil smells slightly musty, it's better to choose another one — it might already have root rot. The leaves should be in good condition with no film or powder on the leaves, no webs or areas that are brown or chewed (obvious signs of pests). Bulbs should be clean, dry, with no damage or mold and they should feel firm. Seed packets should be dry, well sealed, and not past their sell-by date. Again, stating the obvious.

Always examine a plant carefully before you buy. You grab a clematis, thinking that it will have dark blue flowers, and get hold of a purple one. That isn't the end of the world, of course, but you wanted dark blue. You can only get it right by looking closely at the labels.

The best time for plant buying in the cooler growing zones is late spring (May), when the ground is frost-free and the plants can be put outside without fear of them being exposed to cold. Farther south, April might be the best time. Check at your local garden center if you're in doubt.

When you buy plants (other than bedding plants, or annuals), they are usually labelled with a tag that tells about the plant and the conditions it needs. Look on the tag for the zone number (climatic region). If you don't know what climatic zone you live in, ask the staff at the garden center.

Checklist for finding out what you want

Hang on — what kind of a plant do we actually want to buy? Perhaps we should know a few basics before we get into the shop. Then we'll have an idea whether or not we really want to get to know the plant. At least we'll know the basics: what it's called, how old it is, where it lives, and what music it likes.

How long will it live?
Some plants, mainly summer flowers and climbing plants, such as marigolds and sweet peas, only live for one year in the garden (annuals). Personally, I buy them, enjoy them, and then forget about them. Others, such as wallflowers (p. 85) live for two years (biennials); in the first year it's all they can do to grow their leaves and they only flower in the second year. Then there are plants that live for more than two years (perennials). Ivy, for example, can easily live for 80 years. These include trees, shrubs, bulbs, and perennials (sometimes called "herbaceous perennials"). Trees and shrubs have woody trunks and branches. Some lose all their leaves every winter (deciduous), or do not lose them all at once (evergreen), but all put out new shoots and grow again every spring. Most perennials lose their stems and foliage each fall and re-emerge the following spring with new shoots. Perennials must spend the winter in the right location, either indoors or outdoors. There is more about overwintering on pages 30–31.

How big will it grow?
... 4 inches like daisies or 40 feet like knotgrass? Will they grow slowly, like the cherry laurel (because I don't have much space) or quickly, like scarlet runner beans, (because I want to have something pretty to look at as soon as possible)?

Where should it live?
Where the plant comes from is important in determining how it will grow in your particular environment. If it comes from the Mediterranean or the southern U.S., like the cherry laurel, then the balcony needs direct sunlight. If it lives in woods, like clematis, it will grow best in damp, shaded soil with dappled light or semishade on the flowers.

What sort of weather and how much space plants need is always the first thing that gardening books mention, and sometimes this information is also on the labels that come with the plants. The meanings of "sun" and "shade" are obvious. "Semishade" means that the plant should not be in the sun all day long.

How will it survive the winter?
(There's more about overwintering on pages 30–31.)

What is it called?
Plants have common names (poppy, for example) but they also have a scientific or Latin name. Unfortunately, there is no way around this, because the scientific name is the most reliable guide and the only guarantee that you will get in the store what you found in the books. Common names are often not specific enough. Poppies are not just poppies. For example, the corn poppy (scientific name *Papaver rhoeas*) is quite different from Oriental poppy (*Papaver orientale*). The first is a summer flower and only lives for one year. The second is a perennial that dies back and grows again every year. For this reason, scientific names are given in all plant descriptions (even in *Basic Gardening*).

That's it. At least for the basics. So let's go shopping. But watch out, spending spree alert!

9

water

rain

soil

granola

chlorophyll

seeds

air

time

fertilizer

compost

bees

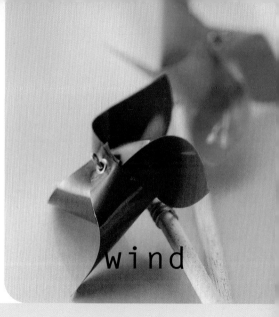

wind

sun

The 14 basic elements for existence

Whatever you need to make the green shoots appear

bulbs

Water

Water circulates through plants in a huge and complex system of veins. Water dissolves the nutrients in the soil, which has to be softened or it would be as inedible as dry oatmeal. It enters the plant via the roots and works its way up. Like the restaurant service elevator in a skyscraper it takes the delicious menu of carbon dioxide, potash, and phosphorus right up to the plant cells on the fiftieth floor. The plant has a trick for overriding gravity. The upper leaves evaporate water, creating a suction effect that draws the water upward again — as if someone were sitting with a drink in front of them and the plant was the straw.

Soil

Believe it or not, there isn't much dirt around. If you subtract the oceans, mountain ranges, permafrost, and deserts, there is only about two and a half acres of farmland left per person. Every living thing on dry land survives on this 12-inch-thick layer. Soil consists of small mountain ranges that have been broken up over millions of years by wind and weather, as well as the discharge from volcanoes and the organic waste of billions of plants and animals. What gardeners love most is loam or humus, soil that is made fertile by the microorganisms that tirelessly decompose dead matter and convert it into fresh soil. There are around 4 trillion bacteria and 80,000 earthworms living in each square yard of soil.

Granola freaks

This is not an insult, it is a badge of pride for all those who are committed to separating their garbage into organic and non-organic, environmentalists and unconventional gardeners who dispense with all poisonous weedkillers, at least in their window boxes or miniature city gardens. We are more interested in creation than destruction. Granola freaks in the *Basic Gardening* sense are all those who do not get rid of every insubordinate dandelion, who spray aphids away with water, instead of bombarding them with the equivalent of cruise missiles, and who in general don't freak out just because something is not growing the way they want, but in some other way and in some other place, or just not at all.

Rain

There wouldn't be much rainfall if plants weren't producing it through evaporation. A birch tree, for example, transpires up to a hundred gallons of water on a hot day, enough to fill a bathtub. In forests, millions of gallons float upward, turn into clouds, and then fall again as rain. The seas are only responsible for about a quarter of all the rain that falls; all the rest is produced by plants! That's why preserving the rainforests is so important. Without the rainforests, the whole world would suffer from drought. The plant-rainfall cycle is a perpetual cycle that makes all the more impact when it pours down in buckets and you left your umbrella at home.

Chlorophyll

Chlorophyll is only found in green plants (mushrooms don't have any). The green color is good to look at and calming for the soul. Why? Perhaps because it has much to do with the sun. Sunlight takes around eight minutes to filter through to the soil and plants but only a fraction of a second to set the energy factories of the leaves — the chlorophyll molecules — in motion. If the sun is shining, plants turn their leaves toward it, to expose as much of their surface area as possible. The chloroplasts, as the chlorophyll cells are called, move quite quickly to where the action is, so as to be able to soak up as much sun and energy as possible. Just like us when we vacation in Florida.

Seeds

This is where it all begins. There are about a quarter of a million species of plants that propagate by seed. All seed embryos (this isn't anthropomorphism, this is the correct botanical name) have a protective covering, some thick and fleshy, such as pomegranate arils, others thin and tough, such as the skin, shell, and husk around a walnut. It's hard to imagine that real plants will grow from the contents of the little packets on the garden center shelf. And that's why you should definitely try growing plants from seed. It's fun to watch living plants come up from tiny seeds buried in the ground. And with just a little watering, they grow and grow and grow.

Air

Everyone wants the cleanest air possible (smokers outside please!) — and plants are no different. First of all, they want plenty of air to breathe, so they don't like being planted too close together. Besides that, it is best for them if the air and climate are as similar as possible to their home environment. This means hot days and hot nights in the tropics, hot days and cool nights in the Mediterranean and California, and plenty of rain in Seattle. The air that we need to breathe is a by-product of plants, since they breathe in carbon dioxide and breathe out oxygen. The oxygen content in the air (21%) is derived exclusively from plants.

Time

In particularly short supply nowadays and not something that will ever increase. We all need it urgently. If plants are to grow in peace from a tiny shoot, they also need time. For many things, timing is all-important. You must plant seeds at just the right time (hoping they will eventually germinate). And gardeners need time — time for their hobby, time to spend in the garden. Even if you have low-maintenance plants, you may still have to bring them inside in the winter or give them a good feed of compost or fertilizer, or apply a mulch — all those things that are important if they are to thrive.

Fertilizer

In the virtual world of the window box, fertilizing is vital, as the nutrients in the soil will be exhausted at some point. There are organic fertilizers (animal manure and worm castings, for example) and chemical fertilizers (artificially manufactured). The difference is that organic fertilizer conditions the soil because it changes only gradually into edible nutrients. Artificial fertilizer, on the other hand, gives the soil what it needs directly, but all at once. The risk is that the plant will be over-fertilized and thus susceptible to disease, and that the soil will become inactive.

Compost

A compost heap is a must for gardeners on the organic kick and the perfect way to naturally recycle everything we usually throw away, such as eggshells, coffee grounds, tea leaves, vegetable parings. The only no-nos are meat and animal or human waste. The material decomposes particularly quickly in a composter, where billions of micro-organisms make fresh, sweet-smelling nutritious soil out of it. Spread it over the old soil like a valuable carpet, giving it a new lease on life, and your plants will grow even more luxuriantly.

Bees

Birds do it, bees do it, even educated fleas do it. We have the bees, rather than the birds and the fleas, to thank for lovely crunchy apples, because they carry the pollen from one plant to the next. This is called pollinating and it is particularly important for fruit trees, since they are lazy pollinators. They can't achieve much on their own and without the bees to do their work for them, we would not have much fruit to eat. The crop is successful if the right varieties of fruit tree are planted next to each other and there are a lot of bees around. That is why professional gardeners place beehives next to their fruit trees, to ensure a really lavish crop.

Wind

The wind fulfills the same function as bees, blowing the pollen and seeds all around – sometimes even onto an adjacent property, where a lawn fanatic will become furious at the weeds spoiling the smooth expanse of grass (or a Basic Gardener will appreciate having some nice surprise guests). The wind is certainly an ally, but it can get on the nerves of city gardeners with drafty balconies. Some plants simply cannot thrive in the wind. If there is any mention of a "sheltered location" on the plant label, you should take it seriously. Plants that are badly buffeted react by nervously shedding their leaves.

Sunshine

The sun supplies the energy for all the super-complicated biochemical processes that take place in plants. Look upon it as a solar cooker that plants use for cooking their meals. The end-product is oxygen and sugar. The conversion process is known as (Greek for "assembling with light"). No photosynthesis, no plant food; no plant food, no oxygen; no food for plants, so no animals and no human beings. (Tip for sun-worshippers: you can find amazing pictures of the sun at the Stanford University website: http://solar-center.stanford.edu).

Bulbs

Bulbs are storage cupboards for nutrients. Flowers that grow from bulbs — such as tulips and lilies — grow again from scratch every year, because during the winter when their leaves die back they have an underground provision store. Bulbs should be planted with the wide end down and twice as deep as they are wide. They sprout in spring and bloom a few weeks later. (There are summer- and fall-blooming bulbs as well, but many of the common flowers, such as tulips and daffodils, bloom in spring.) Eventually, the whole plant above ground withers and turns yellow. Don't cut off the leaves straight away, let them die back completely, then trim away the remains.

The 14 basic elements for existence

Whatever you need to make the green shoots appear

Straight into the pot!

You've had fun plant shopping. And now it's time to plant yourself on the deck chair and the daisies in the pot.

On Saturday, you went shopping, but you just didn't have time during the week to plant your new purchases. However, being a nice person, you wouldn't let them stand out in the blazing sun, in a draft, or in the rain. Until you can plant them, leave them in a sheltered location. Moving is very stressful for plants too.

Please feed!

The most important thing when planting is to use the right soil. Good soil contains many nutrients and it doesn't stick together like cement when it gets wet. The best soil for plants in pots is potting mixture; soil taken straight from the garden is usually unsuitable.

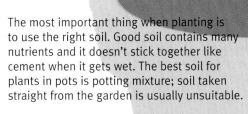

Most potting mixtures contain vermiculite, perlite, and peat moss. The mixture is prefertilized and has been sterilized to kill off fungi that could harm your plants. Special potting mixtures are also available. These include a rhododendron or azalea mixture for plants that prefer acid soil (page 17), sandy mixtures for cacti and many wild flowers, and special mixtures for roses and citrus.

Don't just buy the cheapest potting mixture you can find. The roots of pot-dwellers soon fill their pots, and you shouldn't be sparing with their food. How do you make sure you are buying the right kind of mix (experts call it the "substrate") at the garden center? It couldn't be simpler; they are all labeled on the packaging. You just can't go wrong.

People who think of themselves as "granola freaks," or environmentally friendly gardeners (page 12) will buy soil that does not contain peat moss, but uses a substitute. Peat is created by the decomposition of plants in marshy areas and is used in many potting mixtures to help retain moisture. Unfortunately, the marshes have to be drained to be able to get at the peat, destroying the natural habitats of countless flora and fauna. So it's better to buy other types of potting mixture that consist of renewable raw materials, such as coir. Coir potting mixture is also available in compressed form, a great advantage for people who are not keen on shlepping heavy sacks of soil up to the fourth floor in a building without an elevator. You can buy it in small packs that are as light as a feather. When you soak in water, it swells up and you end up with bucketfuls of it.

The skinny on flowerpots

The plastic pots plants are sold in are often too small for them and the plants should be repotted as soon as possible. You are now faced with which kind of flowerpot to choose. Should you use a planter, a tub, a trough, or a bucket? Should the container be made of clay, plastic, concrete, wood, or metal, regal marble, tasteful terra-cotta, or a pair of your favorite worn-out hiking boots? The answer is it's all a matter of taste. But there are a couple of rules you must stick to. Whatever container you choose (except for aluminum guttering, see page 126), it must have a thumb-sized hole in the bottom for excess water to drain away. Otherwise, the plants will be standing in the wet. This is called waterlogging, or "wet feet" — and it can do a lot of harm. If you are determined to use a container that does not have a hole, however (perhaps an old zinc bucket), you must put a few pieces of broken clay tile or pot in the bottom, so that excess water can collect underneath them. You will still need to be careful not to over-water.

To allow an even flow of water through the container while ensuring that it does not sweep the soil away with it, you need to install another kind of filter or drainage. To do this, place a 1-or 2-inch layer of marble-sized pebbles (pieces of broken clay pot will do) in the bottom of the pot, and place a drainage mat (from the garden center) over them. Then you can put fresh potting mixture on top.

Out of the pot

Now it's time for the plant to come out of the plastic pot. Shake it out carefully, trim away any broken or slimy roots, and shake off any rotting soil. If the plant won't come out, take a look at the bottom of the pot. Sometimes the roots grow out of the holes and become entangled in each other. What you don't want to hear under any circumstances is the crunching noise that the fine root-ends make when they are being ripped, because it is these capillaries, as they are called, that absorb the plant's food. It is better not to use force; instead turn the plant over and carefully but firmly rap it on the bottom of the pot. It often helps to put the plants and the pot in water for half an hour — then it should slide out easily. Make sure the water is not too cold.

Straight into the new pot

Now repot the plant into the new pot, which you have professionally fitted with drainage, and repack soil all around it. But don't pack the soil to the top. There has to be a watering space of 2 inches or so at the top of the pot, so that water does not overflow, but can gradually seep down through the soil. Finally, press down firmly all around the plant and water it immediately. Adding soluble plant food to the water won't do any harm.

Moving into something bigger

Let's say your plant has grown out of its pot and has to move into something bigger. How much bigger? Well, one or two shoe sizes at the most, or it could get root rot, a condition that occurs when the plant is waterlogged. There are no hard and fast rules for knowing when it's time to repot, as plants grow at different rates and have different requirements. But do it as early in the spring as possible, so that by the summer, the plant has gotten used to its new home, and can concentrate completely on flowering.

Clinging or independent?

Many plants need a little support. These are the main types, from the "real clingers" to "totally independent."

Those in need of TLC
Some plants need a strong shoulder to lean on. These are the creepers that spiral upward over anything that gets in their way. They include wisteria (page 62) and honeysuckle (page 132). You will need a firm trellis for them. It can be home-made or storebought and made of wood, plastic, thick wire, or bamboo.

The clingers
Delicate climbing plants, such as many clematis (page 76) can be tied with string or wire to thin stakes. Once they are established, they will twine around any support, as long as it's not too thick. Very light plants (annuals such as black-eyed Susan, page 76) can also use stable perennials as their climbing frame. Balcony railings can be good climbing aids. (Another style tip — drill hooks around the doors to the balcony, put bamboo stakes in the pot, then wind packaging string around them, over the hooks and around the door. Your creeper will frame the door so that it looks like the entrance to Sleeping Beauty's castle.)

The dependents
Climbers such as climbing roses (page 87) or jasmine (page 45) must be tied to a support. They have long shoots but cannot support themselves, so they are dependent upon the gardener.

The totally independent
Ivy (page 128) or Virginia creeper (page 132) climb completely on their own, using their roots or suckers. Some property owners don't like them, claiming they do damage, so ask before planting them.

Straight into the garden!

You can always move a pot to a different location, but rooted plants do not like the idea of moving again. So make sure you find the right location before planting.

How accurate do you have to be about it? It's up to you. Left-brained gardeners (stronger on planning and control) sharpen their pencils and carefully plan the locations to scale on graph paper, just like designing the interior of an apartment. Right-brained gardeners (stronger on intuition and fantasy) just follow their inspiration.

What the plant wants — and what you want

If plants are to thrive it is important to apply the basics. These are sunshine or shade, protection from rain and wind, and space to expand if they are large plants. They also need the right kind of soil (see "Good dirt, bad dirt," opposite). That is why you will find these basic requirements in every plant description.

What the gardener wants is just as important. The "new kids on the block" must not be located in front of smaller plants, concealing them from view. A new plant may not be suitable for borders as it will outgrow it, but it could be just the thing for the pergola to create privacy there quickly. Herbaceous perennials need a special location in the garden because they disappear in winter and re-emerge in spring, and make sure you don't plant anything on top of them.

Smart gardeners plan so that not all of their plants flower at the same time. Ensure your plants have different flowering times, from the very early snowdrops through to those that bloom in the fall.

But how are you supposed to know which flowers you like best if at the best planting time — early spring — everything on the shelf is still so boringly green? There's a trick to it. Visit garden centers all year round and then you can see the plants as they are flowering. And something else to consider before planting – the colors. Do you want a mixture of brightly colored plants? Or would a long, snow-white strip of plants be even lovelier?

The best time for planting is on days that are not too hot, because hot spells are as stressful for the plants as they are for humans. Avoid late afternoon. Spring is the time for planting shrubs and many annuals, fall is the time for planting trees, bushes, and bulbs that will flower the following year. Grasses and ground covers hate the frost, so sow them well before frost in your area. The same applies to laying turf.

Planting technique

When planting trees and large shrubs, the roots need plenty of space in which to expand, so dig a hole using a large spade (you won't get far with anything small). The hole should be wide enough so that the root ball will fit easily, and deep enough to allow the upper edge of the root ball to be level with the ground. Loosen the soil all around and in the hole to make it easier for the roots to penetrate the soil.

Air pockets in the soil can kill the roots, so you must eliminate any gaps in the soil by watering the plants well immediately after planting ("watering in," to use the technical term). Finally, press down the soil around the plant with your hands or tamp it down with your gardening boots. Especially in dry climates, build up a low rim of dirt around the plant so the water stays in the root zone instead of running off elsewhere.

When planting bulbs, make a hole with a broom handle or use a special bulb planter. If the bulbs are packaged, the label will tell you how deep to plant them. But the basic rule is that the larger the bulb, the deeper the hole. Small bulbs should be planted twice as deep as their own depth and, large bulbs three times as deep. Plant bulbs with the roots downward. Cover them with dirt, press down lightly, and water.

Good dirt, bad dirt

Soil is the most important thing in the garden, because it is vital for plant nutrition. Soil can be sandy or clay, rich or poor, acidic, alkaline, or neutral. Some plants (succulents, for instance) like sand, but most plants want something more nutritious. Luckily, the Basic Gardener does not need to dwell at length on the dirt problem. In city gardens, the soil is rarely very sandy or heavy with clay — it is usually somewhere in between. The crumble test will soon tell you what kind of soil you have. Sandy soil will trickle through your fingers, clay soil will stay in a lump. Anything in between is just fine.

If the soil is too sandy, you can buy compost containing loam and mix it in (it's hard work!). If it is too heavy with clay, you can mix in humus (buy it from garden centers) and rake a layer of leaves about 6 inches deep into the soil. This is called mulching. The leaves decompose, giving the soil a looser texture over time.

Another aspect of soil is something called pH, which is a measure of the acidity on a scale of 1 to 14. Neutral soil has a pH of 7, and most plants will do fine in this type of soil. Some plants, like rhododendrons, like an acidic soil (pH less than 7) and some like an alkaline soil (pH more than 7). You can buy a soil-testing kit. What if your soil is acidic? Don't worry, just plant a rhododendron. If you want to "sweeten" an acidic soil, mix in lime, which is available at garden centers.

Super-soil

Soil with a lot of organic matter (humus) in it is a favorite with organic gardeners. You can buy humus or make it yourself by composting. Compost is the very best fertilizer, because it is swarming with micro-organisms and earthworms, which are continuously turning everything over, converting dead plant matter into food and keeping the soil well aerated. To start composting, collect all the organic household and garden waste. Put it in a composter (available from garden centers) in a shady spot. So what can you put in it? Any plant debris except for seed-bearing weeds (logical), waste such as fruit peels, eggshells, and coffee grounds, but no plastic bags or meat scraps. Warning: if it smells bad, you've done something wrong! The compost will take up to a year to mature. By then all the waste will have decomposed and you can spread the sweet-smelling soil onto the garden. Your plants will love it!

Keeping the soil healthy

If the soil is healthy, you will be happy. Here is how to keep it healthy.
• Never dig it over! You should only dig when it is really necessary, such as when digging a hole for planting, because whenever you turn the soil over, you are transplanting micro-organisms from the deeper layers to the upper ones and vice-versa. The micro-organisms will be in the wrong part of the soil and they won't be able to do their job correctly.
• If the soil develops a hard crust due to heavy rain or fierce winds, loosen it slightly. This is an opportunity to use a favorite tool, the rake (page 34). Simply pull the rake through the soil.
• Do not use chemical fertilizer (page 12). Instead, try to use organic (which can be bought ready-made).
• Don't throw away fallen leaves, use them as a mulch.

Getting more out of it

Buying plants is not difficult, but it's not that hard to grow them yourself. And besides, it's much less expensive and it's a lot of fun. You can look forward to spring and summer and you can live in hope and anticipation — seed shopping in February is the greatest! You don't have to do anything more than put a seed the size of a pin-head in the ground and be amazed that something really grows from it! You get a real sense of achievement from growing things and it's incredibly economical. You can turn the whole balcony into a mass of greenery for a few dollars.

A miracle from a packet

The easiest plants to grow from seed are summer flowers, such as the lovely Swan River daisies (page 136), turbo-charged nasturtiums (page 62), or cheerful sunflowers (page 61). You can also easily grow many delicious vegetables from seed. These include zucchini (page 64), cucumber (page 65), runner bean (page 65), amaranth (page 112), strawberry spinach (page 112), pak choi (page 113). These are a few ideas of what is available.

The ingredients

We already have the basic ingredients for getting more out of our gardens or window boxes — a packet of patience, a pinch of intuition, and a double portion of time. And the most important thing of all — the seed packets — can be bought at any garden center and in many supermarkets. Everything you need to know is written on most packets. The packet will tell you whether the plants need to germinate in the light or the dark (in a closet or loosely covered), how warm they like to be, and how long you will have to wait until a green shoot emerges from the soil. The best seeds for dynamic gardening personalities are pumpkin or arugula, because they are famous for their fast germination — the first leaves emerge within a few days. Seeds suitable for Zen gardeners with endless patience include angel's trumpet (page 49). They take a relaxed three months. A real test of perseverance!

Okay, let's go for pumpkin seeds.

So what you need is special, mild, seed-sowing compost that contains no fertilizer. And you will need to buy a seed tray or individual seedling pots. You can buy various types of inexpensive propagation kits in the stores, even miniature greenhouses with heaters. In any case, they must all have a transparent lid (or a clear plastic bag) that provides a hothouse effect. The lid or bag must not touch the leaves or they will rot.

Seed trays are a good idea if you want to put the plants into your boxes as whole clumps, but not so good if you would rather have individual plants for mixed window boxes. This is because the roots do not grow neatly next to each other, but become entangled and are difficult to separate later when you want to repot them. Biodegradable seedling pots are ideal; later, you can simply put the pots with the tiny growing plants inside them into a larger container.

The time to start seeds for summer flowers is the end of February to March and April. The timing depends on the particular plant and also your climatic conditions. Rely on your local garden centers and information on the seed packets for sowing details. Of course, you should not start sowing biennials until late summer. You sow them, feed them well, put them in a pot or flower bed, help them through the winter — and collect your reward the following year when they flower. Growing biennials is really for gardeners who have a more professional approach. Most of us are lazier and buy our biennials in bloom.

Fill the seedling pots with compost, add the seeds, cover with soil (it will tell you on the packet whether the layer should be thick or thin), press down gently, water lightly (preferably with a spray bottle), cover with a lid or bag, and place on a sunny window sill. Very basic, isn't it?

If you are going into propagation big time and growing a lot of different plants, label the pots.

What next? Now it's time to play the waiting game. And because we are masters of self-control, we will talk ourselves out of rummaging around in the soil every day to see whether any tiny shoots are showing through. Of course, you can have a little peep at them every day, and, you should lift the lid or bag now and again to let in some fresh air, but not too much and preferably only if you spray slightly with water at the same time.

At last!

When the seedlings have grown sufficiently, it's time to put them in their proper place. Moving them is no problem if they're in individual pots, but if there are many in the same container, you will have to throw out a few to make room for the rest. It's a cruel world.

Don't repot too soon! Young shoots are too fragile for re-potting, for example. How things progress depends on the mentality of the Basic Gardener. If you are the rugged type who takes a cold shower every morning, you will probably be continuously exposing your seedlings to fresh air. This can only make them stronger if they are ready for such treatment. If they prefer gentler handling, plant them in larger pots and allow them a little longer on the protected window sill, as a honeymoon period, so to speak. There is no set answer here — you must make these crucial decisions for yourself.

Some things don't change, however. Most plants that will be living outdoors should be put out from mid through late May, at the latest. And if they have the right conditions, they will keep growing and you will be able to enjoy looking at them as you breakfast on the balcony, even if you have to put on a thick jacket to do so.

Making copies

I like my oleander so much — I think I'll make a copy of it. Or maybe I'll make two at the same time!

Seeds aren't the only way to get more plants. There's another way. You can make an exact copy of the original plant, with exactly the same characteristics as the parent plant, simply by getting parts of the plant to grow roots. Clever, or what?

So what will I need to do that?

You will need the same equipment as for growing from seed, plus secateurs and a rooting agent (from a specialist store). You'll also need soap and water for washing your hands carefully before beginning, because the secateurs and your hands must be scrupulously clean so that you do not pass on any bacterial infection to the plant. And then, of course, you need the most important thing — a parent plant that is willing to put a part of itself at your disposal. Or an acquaintance or friend who is willing to put a parent plant at your disposal. Cuttings can be made from bedding plants (such as geraniums), perennials, shrubs, or trees.

Here's how you make copies of a geranium (page 70). Simply snip off a shoot, a lovely healthy one. Not the biggest one in the middle (the main shoot), but one of the side shoots. This is called a "cutting" (because you have cut it off). Simply put it into the soil and you will get a clone of the original geranium. You can do exactly the same thing with oleander (page 44) or angel's trumpet (page 49), whose cuttings do not even need soil for them to start rooting, merely a glass of water. Ivy (page 128) can be propagated from just one single leaf that then roots in soil or even in water. Practical, isn't it?

This is how it works

The basics for taking cuttings are the same as growing plants from seed. Put the cutting into mild seed-sowing compost, keep it warm and in the light (under a transparent lid) and always watered. Some plants are poisonous.

Leftovers Tip

I can only get 10 sunflowers in my window sill propagator. Or a maximum of 10 hollyhocks. But there are still several seeds left in the packet. What shall I do with them? My friends don't want them because they don't have any room either. And it would be heartless to throw them away.

The answer is simple — just keep them until next year! How long plant seeds stay fresh varies, but many have a very long shelf-life (radish seeds can last for ten years). A professional tip for storing seeds is to put them into photographic film containers, seal well, and place them in the freezer. A germination test will show if they are still viable. Soak a few seeds in water for a few hours and place them on damp paper towel. Leave them for a few days under a glass bowl, somewhere that is not too cold and not too hot (not by a radiator), and see whether any shoots are showing.

When you cut them, the poison can get onto your skin and make it red and itchy or get in your eyes if you rub them. So remember to wear gloves.

And where do I take the cutting from?

From the very top
Softwood cuttings are cuttings from very young shoots that have not yet flowered. You simply cut off the delicate tip (from 2 to 4 inches long). It is best to cut off just under a leaf joint. Snip off the leaves so that the plant will concentrate on the roots rather than feeding the leaves. Add the compost — and you know the rest.

From the center
Semi-hardwood cuttings are those with leaves that are not too soft but also not too tough. Take cuttings 2 to 4 inches long from just under the leaf nodes.

Cuttings from a bush or tree are called hardwood cuttings. The time to copy trees is in the fall. Cut off a shoot around 6 inches long off the main stem so that a thin sliver of bark and wood also comes away at the base of the cutting. Remove the lower leaves. Nip off the growing tip and dip the base in root hormone. Now plant the cutting half-way into the soil.

From the leaf
Simply snip off a leaf, put it in the soil, and apply slight pressure so that it makes contact with the soil (press it down with a marble, for instance). Or simply place it in a glass of water and wait until you can see roots. This works very well with ivy.

From the very bottom
For bulbs, through bulblets. This often happens naturally, in that the bulbs start growing small side-shoots, so-called bulblets. This is how narcissi multiply in the garden. It is more difficult for a gardener to take bulb cuttings because you need a lot of soil and it only works with a few plants, such as tulips (*Tulipa kaufmanniana*, page 75). When flowering is finished and the leaves are gone (page 30), in summer or early fall, it is time to dig out the bulbs, take off the bulblets, and store them indoors in a dry, warm, dark location. Then dig them back in the garden in October.

To take root cuttings for bushes or trees, cut off a piece of root quite high up and divide it into 2-inch lengths. Place these horizontally in the soil (or place them quite deep, so they are covered), then sprinkle some soil over them. Use this method for roses and oleanders.

For shrubs, propagation is through root division. The best time for this is in the spring, or whenever the plant has grown too big and the roots are almost forcing the pot apart or new shoots are coming out of the soil nearby. Dig out the plant or remove it from the pot. Carefully pull the roots apart, separating them by vigorous shaking (or if necessary with shears or a spade), and plant both parts in fresh soil. This works very well with plants of the saxifrage family, such as astilbe (page 88).

Just keep trying everything. Something is bound to work.

How lazy people can get more lazy

Growing things is quicker and success is guaranteed if you simply walk into a nursery and buy young, individual plants. Even more convenient is plant propagation through the mail. The plants will arrive specially packed and well rooted (page 8). All you have to do then is repot them into bigger pots or put them straight into the garden.

How very lazy people can get even more lazy

Scatter bird seed — the next year you will very probably have a sunflower out there, a surprise guest that will have grown all by itself.

Wellness

Health and fitness are the most important things to me. Here's an extract from my training program for a Saturday in June.

After breakfast: a slow workout
Fetch watering can, into the kitchen, fill with water, back to the balcony, water plants, back into the kitchen, fill with water, back to the balcony, water plants, and so on, at least ten times.

Late morning: walking
Fresh out of fertilizer, so walk to the car, and off to the garden center...

Stretching and Yoga
...fish for a bottle of fertilizer on a top shelf and practice humility by standing in line at the check-out for at least half an hour.

Mid-day: power step
Have to get the oleander that somehow found its way into my shopping cart up the stairs.

Afternoon: spinal gymnastics and weight-lifting
Bend down, pull off dead flowers, up again and throw them out, bend down and get rid of aphids, up again, and throw them away, and so on, at least ten times. Then mix fertilizer in a $2\frac{1}{2}$-gallon watering can full of water, lift, and pour.

Evening: fatburner
Place sausages on the barbecue and cook until crunchy. Take a deep breath and taste. That's all for today!

Like us, plants must be fit and healthy. There are a few minimal conditions if plants are to grow well. And you will find all of the basics for healthy plant growth on the following pages.

Watering and fertilizing

Watering? What's there to know?
You just pour water over them and that's all there is to it!

That's partly true. There isn't that much to it. But you mustn't water too much or too little. And not too often but just often enough. The water mustn't be too hot or too cold. And you mustn't let the roots get waterlogged. Here are the Basics.

The type of water
Tap water — but let it stand for a while — is good for almost all plants, but not quite all. Some plants, including rhododendrons and citrus, like soft water that contains no lime. (You can get a lime remover in gardening centers.)

How much is needed?
There is no standard amount. For example, sunflowers are always very thirsty, but boxwood likes a very small amount of water. It doesn't do any harm to let most plants dry out now and then, as long as you give them a proper soaking afterward. But given too little all the time is bad — most plants will drop their leaves and at some point they will die of thirst. Too much of the good stuff, however, is even worse — too wet is a death sentence! Waterlogged roots cause more fatalities than drought. If you want to be absolutely sure, place a moisture indicator in the soil. But there's always an exception to the rule, even this one. This time it's oleander — it loves being knee-deep in water.

When and when not to water
Water more in summer, much less or even hardly at all in winter. Water in the morning or early evening. Don't water in the blazing mid-day heat. The moisture will evaporate immediately and the drops act like a magnifying glass on the leaves, exposing them to sunburn. Watering too late in the evening is also bad because fungal diseases can take hold on damp leaves in the cold night air and slugs are drawn to the plants as if by magic.

How to water
It's best to water directly onto the soil (except for plants that like to take a shower). Water potted plants until the water runs out of the bottom of the container. In summer do not use ice-cold straight from the tap — let it stand for a few hours so the temperature shock won't be so great for plants in containers.

Erica's flower hotel

And what if you want to go on vacation? A weekend isn't so bad, but two weeks with no water? And the most effective method (friends and neighbors) won't work, because they're away too. But your plants can survive even this, because a whole host of smart watering systems are available from garden centers, both for balconies and gardens. Here are some ideas.
• for weekends, there is the good old woolen thread trick; place a large pot of water next to the plant, hang threads in it, and trail them over the plant
• special, inexpensive containers with a water reservoir
• watering mats
• kits for window boxes with sensors that regulate the dryness and several openings for inserting them into the soil
• for the garden, porous hoses (soaker hoses) that you attach to the tap (just slightly open) and that spray drops of water along their length
• for high-techies there are hoses with sprinkler attachments that are controlled by a timer — this way, you can water your entire city garden

But whatever you choose, test it out before you leave on your vacation.

Plants must be fed

How do you feed plants? Isn't it all written on the bottle? Just pour it into the water and off you go. Isn't that it?

Right again! Just make sure it is the right type of fertilizer for the particular plants and that you are feeding them the right amount in the right season.

Fertilizing container plants

There are two types of fertilizer, chemical and organic. Organic fertilizer is quite simply animal or plant waste, and from an organic gardener's point of view, it is the healthiest for both plants and the environment. Chemical fertilizer is considered by many to be not as good for the soil (page 12). It goes without saying that you should use only organic fertilizer on fruit and vegetables.

Container plants need a good feed more than most. They are growing in cramped conditions in too little soil, so the energy has to come from somewhere. The easiest method is liquid fertilizer in bottles, which is good for almost all potted plants. We recommend using an organic liquid fertilizer. It will have an immediate effect. Follow the instructions on the label and dissolve it in water. Some plants, such as rhododendrons and azaleas, citrus, boxwood, and roses, need special types of fertilizer.

If you have put your plants into fresh potting mixture, wait for around six weeks before using fertilizer. The fresh soil will have a good store of nutrition and minerals.

When to fertilize

Fertilize when the plant is "working," when it's actively growing and flowering, mostly during the summer months. As we know from our own bodies, when we are physically active, we get very hungry.

How much to use

The correct dosage will be on the bottle, but if you're not sure, always use too little rather than too much! If you give the plant too much goodness, it will become susceptible to disease.

How often to fertilize

This varies from plant to plant and is one of the items discussed in the plant listings. If you really want to do it properly, you can pin a reminder on your noticeboard. But those who are lazy by nature can make life easy with one simple rule — apply fertilizer once every two weeks. As a rule of thumb, that will do for most plants. Exceptions are cacti, succulents, and ferns, which should only be fed every four weeks. "Strong feeders," such as geranium and oleander, need feeding once a week during the growing season.

Using fertilizer outdoors

Do you need to feed plants in the garden too? Of course, because the soil outdoors can also become exhausted. Then you need to replace the nutrients that the plants have extracted. That is more important for vegetable gardeners, though, who want to grow huge potatoes. Potatoes are "strong feeders" that take so much nutrition from the soil that you shouldn't plant them twice in a row in the same spot. Vegetable gardeners should use organic compost to fertilize their food crops.

Training and pruning

Wild can be beautiful. But if things get too wild, you could be in over your head — literally!

Of course, you could take a radical, fundamentalist attitude and say, "I will cut nothing back. Things can grow here in total freedom!" But two years later, at the most, you'll be wondering why it's still so dark on the patio in summer. And besides, pruning or cutting back is good for plants, for it enables the whole plant to get the maximum light and air.

Not for pruning

Annuals and biennials die back after flowering, so you don't need to cut them down. Leave bulbs to flower fully and then let the leaves die back until they are brown. The plant draws nutrition from its dying leaves, so wait a few weeks before trimming them neatly.

The kindest cut

Many shrubs do best with at least some pruning. It's best to prune spring-flowering shrubs in May, when they have finished flowering, and evergreen plants and hedges in August, when the birds have left the nest. Roses should be pruned in March or April.

Trimming

Pulling off old leaves and anything that has withered, dead-heading flowers, and cutting off dead branches is an ongoing job.

Some plants are self-cleaning, and they eject their dead flowers. Then again, there are gardeners who enjoy all the snipping and pulling off. There is something satisfying in

ringing in the weekend like that. When it's all done, you feel you have really earned the right to sit down in the sunshine with that steaming cup of coffee.

The golden rules

There are a few basic rules for pruning shrubs and trees, and once you know them you are much less likely to get it wrong.

Why prune anyway?

It's all to do with getting as much light and air to the plant as possible. This makes the plant more resistant to disease.

How to prune

Don't cut the twig or the branch — the technical term is shoot — just anywhere, but as far as possible directly over the small spots in the angle of a leafstalk that have the potential to grow into branches in their own right.

Don't prune horizontally, hold your shears or secateurs at an angle. Make smooth, clean cuts; don't tear at the branch. Only use clean, sharp shears or secateurs. After all, a pruning cut is a wound, so the cleaner it is, the better it will heal. For larger cuts (larger than a nickel) you can buy healing cream.

Weeds and wild plants

"It is the will of Allah," says my friend. "Plants don't come with guarantees. Either they amount to something or they don't."

"It's true. My wallflower never amounted to anything. Instead I got something else that I wasn't expecting. You can call it a weed and be annoyed. Or a surprise and be pleased about it."

My friend has been combining organic gardening and yoga for years and is close to enlightenment. But not everyone can be so cool about weeds and see things that way. For example, I wanted wallflowers. All I got was thistles!

Wild thing

Wallflowers grow in gardens, as well as in the wild. So do wild strawberries and clematis. What is actually so wrong with weeds? After all, all cultivated garden flowers have ancestors that once grew wild. It's a definition thing. Weeds are whatever you don't happen to want in the garden, such as dandelions, speedwell, chickweed, couch-grass, stinging nettles, and even daisies.

How you get on with so-called weeds depends on what type of gardener you are — a conservative one or an unconventional one. Unconventional gardeners think that pumpkins and squash look particularly charming. They have a relaxed attitude to weeds, defining them as "wild herbs" and even planting them (you can buy wild flower seeds). Not only do they not rip weeds out, they even eat them (dandelion leaves in salads, for instance, page 108).

All other gardeners have a tougher time of it, because they have pristine gardens in which nothing is allowed to grow without their permission. These gardeners dig up every-thing that leaves a stump or a stalk and so they have a life's work ahead of them (at least, if they enjoy working like Sisyphus who had to carry his boulder up the hill, carry it up, roll it down, up, down, and so on, forever). When you dig your garden, lots of tiny seeds that might have been waiting for years in the soil to make their ap-pearance come to the surface and shout "yippee!" because you have finally given them the chance to germinate. There is no such thing as spore-free, seed-free, sterile soil once it is in the ground where it is exposed to airborne seeds and spores. Weed killer won't help either.

But even that kind of gardener deserves help. There are a few people who planted wallflowers and that is all they want to see. Just wallflowers. No thistles.

How to get rid of weeds

Where they grow
• In a window box or pot, it is easy to weed by hand.
• In the herb patch: as long as the weed is still young and not too awkward, pull it out by its roots.
• In the vegetable patch and for badly affected flower beds: cover the soil with special black plastic (available from a garden center), make diagonal slits in it, place the plants under these slits, and pull them through. Everything still under the black plastic gets no light and dies.
• Under berry bushes and in flower beds: collect fallen leaves and branches. Or buy ready-made mulch. Spread mulch or green matter in a thick layer over the soil. It will do a lot to keep down the weeds.
• Plant overhanging shrubs, such as peonies, or trees, or ground-cover, or thick bushes. Anything that covers the ground gives weeds less of a chance.
• On the lawn: this is where it is most difficult. If you *must* use weed killer, measure it out precisely, otherwise you will get yellow patches in the grass. That goes for fertilizer with added weed killer too (it's really not necessary).

When to spray
If you're determined to spray, do it in early spring — or at least before flowering.

What to do with them
Don't put seed-bearing weeds on the compost heap. Burn them or put them in the garbage can, otherwise more weeds will grow from the seeds.

How to weed
Pull the whole plant out by hand, by the roots. If you don't get the roots, you're just wasting your time because they will grow again. But please try not to use weed killer chemicals.

Debugging

"My beautiful new sunflower is no more. It's all gone, vanished, eaten away."

All that remains is a single leaf with an astonishingly large bite taken out of it, but all the tiny leaves and the entire bud have gone. A slimy trail vanishes into the jungle. A tragedy has unfolded here. The slugs must go!

But how? Poison is out of the question due to my highly developed sense of environmental awareness. In any case, poison will also kill millions of beneficial micro-organisms. Even slugs are useful members of the food chain. Poisons are just not on with Basic Gardening. And that's that.

There is no easy answer to the problem of the bands of predators (aphids, whitefly, mealybugs etc.) and spider mites (red and black), slimy crawlers (slugs and snails) and mammals (groundhogs, skunks), fungi (rust, smut, mildew) and bacteria (geranium wilt) (page 71). So what should I do?

Well, for the container garden, the poison ban is not so radical. The soil in the pot is isolated, so the chemicals will not affect such a large area. And besides, potted plants need more help because they have a harder time of it in their miniature home than their colleagues living in open beds. Container gardeners can go to the store and ask for the key to the poison cabinet, which will definitely be locked. The experts at the store will only fetch the key if they believe it is the right thing to do.

Fortunately, we also have a few tricks up our sleeve. The most important of these is prevention. In other words, treat the plant right. Put it in the best location, water it properly, and feed it when it needs it so that it is strong and disease-resistant. Prevention also means not starting off on the wrong foot. Earthworms, for example, are beneficial. Roll out the red carpet for them instead of hunting them down — they keep the soil healthy! Butterflies, moths, large spiders, earwigs, lacewings, ladybugs, and many other bugs love to eat the plant pests. We also need them because they fertilize our plants. So, instead of mowing your lawn to within an inch of its life, keep a few islands of wild herbs. These will keep hoverflies, fireflies, ladybug larvae, and many other useful insects around.

It is very practical to exploit natural enmities as much as you can. Small mammals eat slugs. Or try the Buddhist method of disposing of them. Go outside with a flashlight at dusk and gather up slugs and snails from the plants. Put them in a bucket and take them to the local park or outside the city limits. (Not just for ethical reasons, but also because it is really not pleasant killing slugs.)

With many pests, such as aphids, debugging with diluted liquid detergent will do the trick. Just spray the plant with this mixture or with an infusion made from boiling rhubarb leaves (you can even buy this as a powder in organic gardening centers and stores). Or, if the plant can take it, simply hose it down with a powerful water jet.

The flower doctor is on call!

What it looks like and what causes it	What you can do about it
Defoliation and slime trails, particularly in the very delicate shoots? It's time for action. At night, and if it rains during the day, you can blame slugs and snails. Snails are less harmful.	The crafty method: dig in a yogurt pot right to the upper rim, pour some beer into it, and collect regularly; replace the beer after it has rained. Preventative: scatter barricades made of wood shavings, bark, sand, stone dust, lime, crushed eggshells, or pine needles around plants. Additionally: do not discourage large bugs, insect-eating birds, skunks, groundhogs, and toads — they really love snails.
Gnawed, rolled up, or shrivelled buds and shoots. Leaves often sticky, Whitefly and aphids are to blame — they come in swarms in damp springs and summers. Ants are also indirectly to blame. They tend aphids in order to extract the sweet honeydew, and they defend their sweet booty even against aggressive attackers.	Household remedy: spray with horticultural oils. The Buddhist approach: brush them off by hand. Be gentle or you could damage the buds. Preventative: ladybugs, larger bugs, earwigs, spiders, and birds love aphids — so let birds nest, and don't drive away spiders! Or buy organic tomato food. It strengthens the plant and thus prevents pests. For a bad infestation and really only in exceptional cases use a powerful insecticide recommended by your local gardening center. To discourage ants: scatter lavender or ant oil onto ant trails; they hate the smell. Or sprinkle the trails with coffee grounds. Or stick a sheet of copper in their hole — they will emigrate. But don't kill them! Ants eat plant waste and dead animals.
The leaves turn yellow, then brown, then wither. Pale spots on top of the leaves and thin webs indicate tiny spider mites.	Snip off the leaves. Household remedy: spray with garlic tea (pour hot water over 2 garlic bulbs, then add 2½ gallons of water and steep for five hours). Preventative: encourage spiders and ladybugs. Or use an organic pesticide. Mist frequently and make sure the plant doesn't get too hot and has plenty of air. Spider mites love hot, stale air.
There is a white, powdery coating on all parts of the plant above ground. This is a fungus, a powdery mildew. There are two types of mildew, powdery and downy. Powdery mildew attacks roses, delphiniums, and fruit trees; downy mildew attacks vegetables, annuals, and some herbs.	Cut off diseased plant parts. You can try planting garlic between the plants — this keeps vampires away as well. Household remedy: spray with garlic tea (see above). Preventative: when buying plants make sure that they are "mildew-resistant" and that they have enough space around them. You can also buy organic fungicides from specialist stores.
Lumpy brown patches on twigs and branches. Attacks houseplants, fruit trees, roses, and other shrubs. The brown patches are the shells of scale insects that attach themselves to the bark. They remain stationary, but their offspring called crawlers move to their locations.	Preventative: with container plants, the problem is often due to errors in care that weaken the plant and leave it vulnerable to attack. Household remedy: brush off or scrub off with soapsuds. Or buy an appropriate insecticide from a garden center.

When Jack Frost comes to call ...

...it's time for many plants to hibernate. From November through early March, they simply take an enviable break, at least if they are in Canada or the central or northern U.S. In desert regions, some plants take a break and go into suspended animation if there is a dry spell. Other plants may take short breaks throughout the year instead of one long one.

Whenever and however they do it, plants all need a break. The experts call it a "vegetating-break." The plants use this break to gain strength for the coming year. They don't ask for much during this time: just minimal warmth, hardly any water, and no fertilizer. In fact, you should stop feeding most plants in August.

Winter quarters

You will need decent quarters for the plants to enjoy their rest in peace. What that means in practice depends on how tender or how hardy they are. And that, in turn, depends on where they come from and where they are growing. For instance, Mediterranean plants (page 40) growing in a cooler climate need to be overwintered indoors. "Classic plants" (page 66) can stay outside. Information on over-wintering your plants can be found in each plant listing in this book and on the label that comes with the plant when you buy it.

Cold is not the only danger, though. Many plants that don't survive winter do not freeze but dry out. This is especially true of container-grown plants. You have to water outdoor plants now and again, but only on frost-free days (otherwise they will definitely freeze to death), and only sparingly.

A more significant problem in temperate areas with high rainfall is waterlogging. If the drainage is not adequate and the roots become waterlogged, the plant will die.

If you are bringing plants indoors for the winter, snip off all faded blooms and trim the leaves and stems. Do not let them dry out completely during the winter. Water them sparingly if they are kept in a cool place and a little more if they are in a warmer spot.

On mild days, you can let some fresh air into the winter quarters, to prevent fungus diseases, but do so only for short periods. If it is too dry, put bowls of water nearby to increase the humidity.

Don't wave winter goodbye too soon — it often gets in a parting shot that kills off new shoots in the middle of spring. If you think there is a danger of a late frost, cover the plants in the evenings with plastic sheeting. In a cold growing zone, keep them indoors until all danger of frost is over.

From hardy to tender

Couldn't care less
This subject is of supreme indifference to annuals such as sunflowers, which will have died long before winter comes.

Completely hardy
Some plants (small trees and shrubs, herbaceous perennials, and plants grown from bulbs) can survive in the garden without help. Yet even these hardiest of the hardy can be helped with a thick layer of mulch (straw, wood chips, etc.) as a protection against frost. Don't forget to water on frost-free days, if necessary.

Still fairly cool
It is fine to leave many fully hardy container plants in the garden, but not just as they are, because their roots are protected from the icy cold by only a little earth and the thin sides of the container. Container plants do best if you wrap them up nicely in a material such as straw or hay (available in small quantities from pet stores and feed stores), plastic sheeting, burlap bags, or conifer branches. Another method for herbaceous perennials is to place several pots inside one big container, with newspaper underneath and packed into the spaces between the pots. Water them carefully and lay conifer branches over them. Water them with lukewarm water on frost-free days.

Quite a few plants are fine when covered from the top, but only if it's with material that will let the air in. So don't use plastic; use sacking or straw matting instead.

Really quite uncool
Tender plants include many summer-flowering perennials that grow from bulbs or tubers (such as *Canna indica*, page 103). If you live in a colder growing zone, you will have to dig these up and keep them in a box until early the following year. Make sure the location you choose is as dark as possible and cool but not freezing.

Plants accustomed to warm climates — all the species native to the Mediterranean, south and central America, or the tropics — need to come into the house from early October onward if you live in a colder area. Most tender plants require a well-lit, cool place to stay. Of course, the window sill gets plenty of light, but it's too warm there. What about the basement or the garage? The cellar will be too dark and the garage will be both too cold, because it is unheated, and too dark, to say nothing of the car fumes. So you have to look elsewhere. The best place is probably the hallway or the stairwell, where it is usually still fairly light and cool, but not freezing. You could also make do with a spare room or guest room where you can keep the plants at a temperature of about 50°F.

Winter fun

Winter in Canada and much of the eastern, central, and northern U.S. is a forced break for gardeners. A time for self-preservation and plant preservation. But that doesn't have to be bad. Here are a few tips and tricks for winter fun.

• Curl up by the fire with a pile of seed catalogues! And *Basic Gardening* nearby, of course. Enjoy yourself imagining all those things you simply have to try out next summer.
• In early spring, cut a few branches of forsythia and arrange them in a vase. (If you haven't got your own, you could even buy them.) Then you'll get a lovely winter surprise: in the warmth, these apparently naked twigs will start to sprout, and if you're lucky they might even flower.
• Anyone who absolutely insists on having a plant in flower in the winter should get a witch-hazel (scientific name: *Hamamelis*). This lovely shrub produces yellow or red blooms in fall and winter. Plant them between fall and spring in a sheltered position in full sun or semishade. And, of course, there's always poinsettia.
• Great consolation is also available in the form of chives, land cress, chia, chervil, basil, and arugula, which can be grown in little pots on a warm, well-lit window sill. Simply sow the seeds and soon you'll be harvesting vitamins!

watering can

spade

shears

The **green**

17

Basic
hardware
for
Basic Gardening

hose

hoe

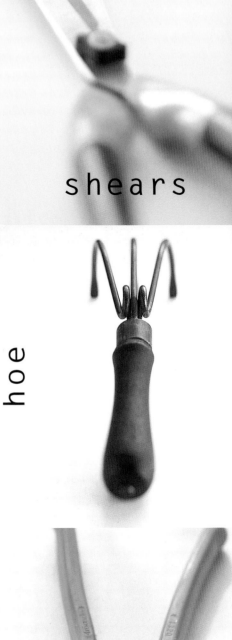

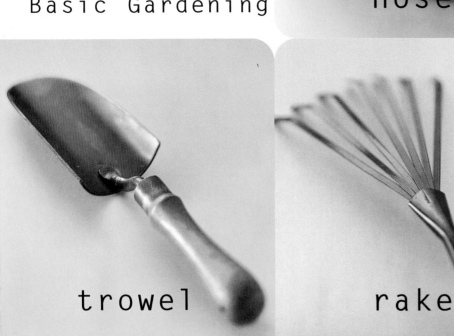

trowel

rake

secateurs

pots

wire

gloves

bamboo canes

basket

raffia twine

hook

pebbles

...that's all
you need

Watering can

A valuable tool — just don't get one that's too small, or you'll be constantly running back and forth and nothing will get watered properly. Some plants, sunflowers for instance, are real heavy drinkers. So the can should hold at least 1¼ gallons, or better still 2½ gallons. Another important point: if the opening in the top is too big the water will spill out, but if it's too small, it will take too long to fill. You will also need a "rose" attachment for plants that prefer to take a shower. If the watering can looks attractive as well (even if it's not an antique), then your happiness will be boundless.

Spade

The Basic Gardener needs one of these in his or her collection to dig holes in the earth, to dig the soil over, to dig out the roots of small trees, or to lay crunchy gravel paths. Or to fill the children's sandbox in early summer and empty it again in winter. Or to heave tightly ingrown plants out of their holes. Some spades are narrow and sharp, others are wide and square, and still others rounded. Those with a T-handle offer a firm grip. You need to be clear about one thing: dirt is not as hard to dig up as people think — it's even harder. Using the spade can be quite a strain, but having the correct one can make the job easier.

Shears

Basic Gardeners prefer hand-trimming to using power saws. It really isn't necessary to cut your boxwood hedge in a precise geometric shape. The best clippers are the ones with a serrated edge rather than a straight one, and a central gearwheel gives a much easier cutting action. Hedge-trimming this way can even be more fun than doing it with a chainsaw (and one wouldn' normally think of "fun" and "hedge-trimming" i the same sentence), because a chainsaw weigh a lot more, is quite hard to hold straight, and isr safe to use with kids around. Hedge-clipping wi "body-power" not only makes you feel better, it really is not as hard as you think.

The green 17 Basic hardware for Basic Gardening

Hose

Always useful, as long as you don't stand on it. You also need a nozzle attachment so that you can adjust the stream of water from accurate and fierce to a nice gentle trickle. In bigger gardens it is useful to have either a movable hose reel trolley, a fixed spray point in the soil to which you can attach the hose, or a soaker hose laid out in the garden beds. This means that you don't have to drag the hose through the flower beds and mow everything down. One more point — someone without much experience using hoses will always get soaked at first. You need to learn how to manage the perverse things. But a soaking doesn't matter in the summer — don't get mad, just get dry.

Hoe

This makes the soil loose and light and can mean the difference between gently loosening it and forcibly digging it over. For example, when planting in beds, using a hoe means you can break up the bottom and sides of your freshly dug planting hole a little. The roots will not encounter a hard wall that will slow their growth, but will be able to spread out unhindered. The Basic Gardener will always have his or her hoe in hand to break up clods of earth. Most hoes have wooden handles and a leather strap for hanging them up, and should last for years.

Trowel

An indispensable basic super-tool for the city gardener. It's certainly true that grubbing in the dirt with your hands is pleasant, no doubt about it. But for digging in balcony planters and flowerpots and for digging out small plant-ing holes, you need something a little tougher. We recommend trowels with a slightly pointed blade because they dig more easily if the earth is a bit on the hard side. Before you buy it, test it first to see if it feels comfortable in your hand, and don't worry yourself unduly about the workmanship — trowels don't break easily. However, if you want to dig deep, you'll need a full-size spade.

Rake

Old-fashioned metal rakes are ideal if you want to level freshly turned soil, for example. But these are not as good for raking up leaves and grass, because bits of wood and other organic matter often get stuck between the prongs and then you have to pull it all out. Bamboo rakes are more suitable for this purpose. By the way, take a good look at the handles. Some sup-pliers offer flexible systems, with one handle — whether plastic or wooden, short or long — that can be used with a rake, a shovel, and a hoe.

Secateurs

It is quite important that secateurs are sharp, because plants don't take kindly to having their stems partly cut and partly torn. You can get short, powerful secateurs for thicker shoots and branches and longer, thinner ones for cutting more tender shoots or trimming a miniature lavender hedge into shape. They should be comfortable to hold, so you don't get blisters when you have to chop up a few thicker branches for the compost bin or garbage can. There are different sizes as well, and special left-handed secateurs. Try them in the store to make sure you get what's right for you.

Pots

om a plant's point of view, the most pressing
ed in a flowerpot is a hole in the bottom so
e plant doesn't become waterlogged. From
e gardener's point of view, we want some-
ing attractive. The standard terra-cotta pots
th a drainage hole are functional enough.
ere are also plastic imitation terra-cotta pots
at look almost genuine but aren't to every-
e's taste. Wooden planters aren't cheap, and
ten require home assembly. Fancy terra-cotta
ots and containers are beautiful, but they are
xpensive and often come without drainage
les. Use your imagination when looking for a
nique, innovative pot. The possibilities are
ndless.

Wire

This is useful when you need something
stronger than twine — for example, when tying
up unruly roses, reinforcing the stems of top-
heavy sunflowers, or quickly fastening
lanterns, aluminum buckets, or other metal
containers to a balcony or trellis. Wire comes
in various strengths. Try to get the wire with
a soft, green, plastic sheathing because it
doesn't cut into the branches as much if you
tighten it gradually. Take care to leave a small
space between branch and wire. Cut wire with
proper wire-cutters. You can also use pliers to
snip off lengths of wire.

Gloves

You really do need these! For example, when
pulling ivy off walls and trees to which it has
anchored itself with an iron grip. Even ordinary
European ivy is slightly poisonous, and without
gloves your hands would itch. You also need
them for cutting roses. Gloves with the longest
possible gauntlets are the best, because the
thorns really grab, stab, and scratch you everywhere. You also need gloves if you are going to
root around in the dirt — which is a shame,
because it's far more fun bare-handed.

Bamboo canes

any plants, such as roses, need some kind
f support to keep them upright. These can be
ticks (for young saplings) or a framework or
ellis. You can easily buy these ready-made
om garden centers. They can be made of
ood, plastic, or bamboo, and they often have
rather dreary appearance. Bamboo is a nice-
oking, easily portable all-round system for
iving support to fast-growing climbing plants.
imply stick the cane into the earth and tie the
lants to it with string, but not too firmly.
amboo doesn't rot quickly and it's fairly
urable. If you add horizontal supporting
anes tied in with string, you will get a pretty
trong framework.

Baskets

Baskets are practical for carrying newly bought
plants, taking fallen leaves to the composter,
and bringing your fruit harvest into the kitchen.
A basket is also a sensible place for the city
gardener to keep all his or her basic tools (they
have to go somewhere, and it's a dreadful
chore to have to run down to the cellar every
time you want to take a single cutting). Baskets
look quite attractive as flowerpot covers. Hand-
woven baskets are particularly beautiful. You
can even use them as planters (bedding plants
look especially good in them), as long as you
first line them with plastic sheeting and moss.

Raffia twine

Twine is used for tying up overgrown plants.
If you want to build a framework for your
plants you can pull some raffia straight across
a balcony and let lightweight climbing plants,
such as honeysuckle, or vines entwine themselves along it. Parcel twine looks okay and is
fairly robust, at least for one summer, but raffia
is better. It is light and discreet, it doesn't rot
quickly, and its knots are easy to untie. Raffia
comes in lots of colors, though green is the
least noticeable. Twine is available from gift-
ware stores in any color and form you can
think of. If you prefer it to be more robust
you can use marine twine, which practically
lasts forever.

Hook

The hook looks like a sickle or scythe but
nstead of being used for cutting down long
grass or grain, it is drawn through the earth on
the end of a long handle. It breaks up the earth
without having to dig it over completely. Of
course, you have to dig the earth over sometimes — to put new plants in, for example.
Many traditionalists dig everything over as an
end in itself, as a sort of annual compulsory
exercise. But today's organic gardeners believe
one should leave the digging-over to the many
tiny living creatures, from microbes to earthworms, that are constantly busy turning all the
organic matter in the soil into nutritious humus.

Pebbles

Stone always looks good, whether it's a small
gravel path to the terrace (don't just spread it
about though — dig a deep-enough base with
straight sides and pack down the edges before
filling it with sand and gravel) or a decoration
on the window sill. Fans of feng shui, bonsai, or
Zen like the presence of pebbes. You can buy
pebbles at garden centers. Pebbles and gravel
help control the amount of water in plant pots.
If you scatter a handful in the base of the pot,
they prevent the hole from getting blocked and
allow excess water to drain out easily.

...and that's all you need

Yes, mowing the lawn is strenuous. A smart
automatic lawnmower with infrared edge-
warning facility will certainly make it a lot
quicker, but it will cost you as much as an
exotic vacation and it cannot really be included
in the list of basic gardening requirements.
Neither can mini-tractors. Even electric lawnmowers come with a warning. They are certainly
easy to use, but then there's always that hassle
with the cable. And gasoline-powered mowers
are a definite no-no. They stink and roar and
turn peace-loving neighbors into ferocious,
deadly enemies. There — do you need any
more persuasion?

Hedges and lawns

Two super-basics: we want a green lawn to lie on and relax, and we want an impenetrable hedge to give us our privacy.

What sort of hedge? There are high ones, low ones, formal ones, casual ones — it's purely a matter of taste. Some people like their hedges as neat as concrete walls. Personally, I prefer them natural and a little wild.

Each type of hedge has its own advantages and disadvantages. Formal hedges take up far less room but they need a lot of work. On the other hand, you can just leave a naturalistic hedge to grow, though it will grow pretty thick and leave trailing ends. Someone who hasn't got much space (and that includes most city gardeners) but nevertheless likes the laid-back hedge look should choose shrubs that will grow neither too high nor too thick. If they also want privacy in the winter, they must get evergreens. Impatient gardeners must go for something that grows quickly. The choice of hedge plants is certainly wide enough.

Formal hedges

These grow fairly tall and have to be properly trimmed. Suitable types include:
• The European hornbeam (*Carpinus betulus*). Good value and requires pruning only once a year. Ideal for gardens with limited space.
• The fast-growing evergreen privet (*Ligustrum*). Ready, steady, go — you'll have a hedge within two years.
• The field maple (*Acer campestre*) is another turbo-powered hedge. Prune it early or its stems will get too thick.
• The evergreen yew (*Taxus baccata*) is the noble-needle hedge (but it is expensive).
• The cherry laurel (*Prunus laurocerasus*) produces luxuriant white panicles and is also good at keeping out exhaust emissions.
• Red cedar, or arborvitae, (*Thuja*) is a traditional and indestructible evergreen for hedging.

Informal hedges

The following shrubs don't grow too big for small gardens or make too much work for the gardener.
• Evergreen berberis (*Berberis* sp.) grows to 10 feet unpruned but can be pruned to half that height.
• Deutzia (*Deutzia* sp.) has white or pink blossoms.
• Spirea (*Spiraea* sp.) grows to 7 feet and has white, pink, and red blossoms.
• Weigela (*Weigela* sp.) produces pink or red flower clusters in May–June and again in fall.
• Sweet briar (*Rosa rubiginosa*) is the best hedge plant. It smells like apple-blossom.

Planting hedges

When to plant
Plant deciduous hedges in March–April or in October–November.
Evergreen hedges should be planted in August–September, as they need time to root.

How to plant
Dig out a hole that is wide and deep enough for the roots of the shrubs to fit in comfortably, and do not leave much space between plants.

Pruning hedges

When to prune
Deciduous hedges need pruning twice a year, first in June (no earlier, as birds are still nesting in them) and then again in February–March.
Evergreen coniferous hedges, such as yew, are slower growing so they only require an annual pruning in July.

How to prune
First, trim both sides so that the top is narrower than the base. This allows light in at the base of the hedge, so it doesn't become leafless at the base. Cut from the base toward the top so that the offcuts won't keep falling on you. In colder areas, leave the corners rounded rather than angular, so that any winter snow will simply slide off and not weigh the hedge down.

To finish, cut the top section horizontally (perfectionists stretch out string and cut along it, but laid-back gardeners cut it as best they can and are quite happy with the results). With young hedges, cut back the new growth by about half, so the hedge doesn't shoot up too fast and produce sparse lower growth. Prune it again in August.

Lawns

As with hedges, there is a variety of style. You may want a formal English lawn that feels like an Italian haircut and radiates the nobility of the golf course. Others dream of wild meadows full of poppies, cornflowers, yarrow, and corn-cockle... Again, each has its advantages and disadvantages: looking at wildflower meadows is indeed pleasant, but you can't trample all over them because it threatens them with destruction. Formal lawns are for nothing other than walking on, but require care and attention.

Buying a lawn

You can buy prepared lawn mixtures containing a variety of grass seeds, or you can have an individual mixture made up. On offer are English super-grass (for those with delusions of grandeur), fine ornamental grass (a lifetime's work), play- or sports-grass (which stands up well), and basic everyday grass (which can really be used). As far as seeds go, don't spare the expense!

For the impatient, lawns can be bought ready-made from the garden center, in the form of long rolls of turf. The grass is growing in a layer of humus 6 inches thick. You can simply roll it out to fit the space, just like a carpet.

New lawns

Anyone buying a new house will find that the garden plot consists of nothing but fresh, bare earth. This can be turned into a lawn very quickly:

When to plant
The best time is from April through June, but August and September will also do.

How to plant
First of all, tear out any sprouting thing that you do not want, rake the ground level, and tread it down with boards or a lawn roller (available for rent at home and garden or tool rental centers). Wait for about two weeks and then pull up anything else that shows its head.

Water the area thoroughly the day before you sow the seeds. Since the packet often contains a mixture of seeds, give them a good shake so that they will be distributed evenly. It's best to sow on dull, cloudy, windless days. Scatter the seeds, rake them gently into the soil, and sprinkle them lightly with water. Water the new lawn lightly every day for the next two weeks, even if it rains continuously. Don't let it dry out! You'll be able to walk on it four to six weeks after sowing.

Old lawns

If you already have an unsightly old lawn, you will have to get rid of it. Simply turning the earth over is not going to work. In fact, it is quite harmful, because it will turn up a matted layer that won't let any water through. Grass can even stop growing on old lawns.

A rototiller that tears up the ground is helpful in cases of radical lawn restructuring (you can rent them from tool rental places). But you will have to collect and dispose of any plant remains after using it.

Put down new soil and follow the guidelines for new lawns (see above).

Mowing the lawn

It's a moment of great satisfaction when the grass is about 3 inches tall and your mower goes into action for the first time (for this first mowing, adjust the blades so that only the tips of the grass are cut). Regular mowing is good for the lawn because it stimulates growth. Don't cut it shorter than 2 inches or the lawn will dry out too quickly.

Feeding the lawn

Lawn roots only go down to a depth of 6 inches, and it grows close together, so it will clearly need quite a lot of feeding. We recommend applying an organic fertilizer in May. (Organic types stay active longer and are good for the micro-organisms in the soil.) Or you can buy special lawn fertilizers. Apply the fertilizer again in July.

Improving lawns

Moss will grow wherever there is standing water, so if you prefer grass, apply algae and lime moss-killer and rake the lawn occasionally to remove the matted grass. If it's especially bad, only the rototiller will help (see "Old lawns"). That ought to clear up the problem!

Plants

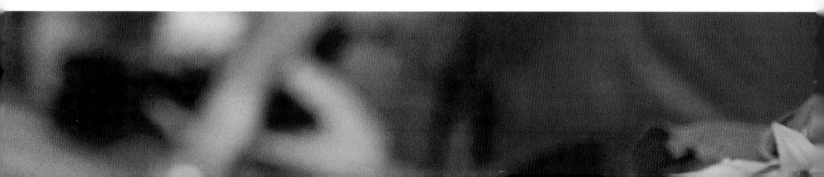

Medite

Everything you need to live the dolce vita at home

rranean

There's something missing in summer if you can't vacation by the sea. Unless you live in California or Florida, you'll need to get away, and maybe even if you live there, a trip to the Mediterranean is an eye-opener. The sounds and smells of the Mediterranean — the buzz of cicadas and crickets, the bustle of the harbor, the scent of jasmine mingling with that of charcoal-broiled meats and engine oil, and the brilliant light that the Impressionist artists loved so much are all there waiting for you.

Coming home is something of a downer. You may be greeted by rain and wind, and Hurricane Harold. You'll long for the sights, sounds, and smells of the sunny South.

But you can re-create the Mediterranean right in your own backyard or balcony. There's surely room for a small lavender or oleander bush or even an olive tree in a tub to conjure up green memories of your summer idyll.

Oh dear, ice-cold hands...

The olive tree sheds its leaves in winter in a cool climate. It won't look too good in the hall, in fact it looks awful. So you put it away in some dark corner where you won't be constantly reminded of this disaster and sidle past it with a guilty conscience. And then, spring has hardly arrived and it's putting out new shoots. Thank goodness! You haven't ruined it. How come? Because unlike most Mediterranean plants that like to be in a cool but bright spot in winter, olive trees can tolerate a cool dark place. You just need to know that. And to think you almost threw it away!

Snow and ice are a problem for Mediterranean plants, as winters are fairly mild, except on the mountaintops. A true Mediterranean plant cannot tolerate the harsh winters of, say, New England or the Great Plains. So for a Mediterranean garden design you have to take into consideration the cold conditions that prevail in growing zones 1 through 6. That means doing your homework to find out what conditions will enable plants to survive the winter.

Don't take them home

When plant lovers on vacation see luxuriant displays of greenery in Andalucia, Spain or Tuscany, Italy or elsewhere in the Mediterranean, they get itchy fingers. Digging them up and taking them away is not a good idea and, in any case, it is illegal to import live plants into the U.S. and Canada. But the packages of seeds available at airport gift shops in Greece, Spain, Italy, etc., can be imported.

Buy the seeds, take them on the plane, but beware when you get them home. I write from experience: 99% of plants from southern climates don't survive and even if they do, they don't grow well.

Whether it's an olive or an oleander, it's better to buy plants from the local garden center, as they will already have been acclimatized to your conditions.

Fragrance

All over Provence, you can buy the lavender scent of the Mediterranean in virtually every form, lavender soap to lavender honey. Lavender is quite hardy and flourishes in temperate and cool climates, so try your hand at putting it to good use.

Lavender water:

1 Take two cups of lavender flowers from the garden and pour 1 quart of boiling distilled water over them. Stir, cover, and leave to macerate for 48 hours.

2 Strain the mixture through a sieve. Squeeze the flowers well, add 2 tablespoons of vodka, and pour into small bottles.

Incidentally, Queen Victoria used to sprinkle it onto her handkerchief and inhale it when she felt stressed— it is said to be tremendously revitalizing.

For novelty gardeners I
Capers

In Greece capers grow like weeds on every wall and pathway...

The Greeks gather capers growing wild, pickling them in vinegar or sea salt, then using them as herbs. (Beware if you follow their example, because scorpions like to hide among the caper leaves.)

If you want to grow capers in North America, you must be prepared to experiment and be inventive, patient, and very optimistic. *Capparis spinosa* demands growing conditions that are as close as possible to its native environment: stony soil with plenty of limestone and a lot of sunshine. The first two are available here (rockery plus an extra portion of garden lime and sand mixed into the soil; you can buy this from a local store). But the sunshine could be a problem.

If you succeed, the lovely pale lilac and white flowers will be a feast for the eyes and the pea-sized flower buds (capers) can be pickled or salted. And if it all goes wrong, pickled capers are available at the supermarket (minus the scorpions!).

Herbs in an oil can

You've struck oil, but only for growing herbs

How

Let's copy the Greeks and plant herbs and flowering plants in these really stylish large metal cans in which they export olives or olive oil. (Don't forget to put holes in the bottom.)

Where

You can buy imported olives or olive oil in these attractive cans in gourmet stores and Greek delicatessens (full of course — first you have the task of gradually using up the superb contents). If you are lucky enough to live in a city with a substantial Greek population, any local grocery store should have them.

Styling Tip

I need some notion of the ocean!

The most important thing about the seaside is — the sand!

It can really bug you when sand sticks to your beach towel and creeps into every nook and cranny of the car. But there's something missing without it too. And a little bit of it in the garden or on the balcony gives you that Mediterranean feel-good feeling. A thin top layer of sand in the lavender pots (p.45) or in an olive-tree tub is immediately reminiscent of southern climes. You should definitely extend this positive reinforcement of the holiday feeling right through the inside of the house. Give unexciting window sills and flowerpots the Mediterranean touch by festooning them elegantly with bits and pieces from the shore. Our window sills are covered with stones, seashells, driftwood, pine cones — all gathered during our various seaside vacations.

For novelty gardeners II

Wild Fennel

Wild fennel seldom comes singly! *Foeniculum vulgare* has the ability to seed itself, so it spreads like wildfire. If fennel is sown in the spring, the strong stems with yellow blooms will grow to a height of six feet. When rubbed, the leaves smell strongly of aniseed.

In the Mediterranean and California, wild fennel grows like weeds. It loves the sun and the strong, salty, sea breeze (which carries its seeds far and wide). Of course, fennel can be used in cooking (delicious with fish), but for the novelty gardener, the feathery leaves add interest as the highlight of garden beds and balcony containers. This Mediterranean example is different from many of its fellow subtropical plants because it is quite uncomplicated. It can withstand harsh winters and doesn't require any special soil type in order to grow in profusion. It prefers to be fairly near the sea, however.

43

Oleander

O sole mio! O leander!

What it is:
- a shrub with magnificent blooms ranging in color from white to deep red
- can tolerate cold conditions ...
- ... but not a hardy plant (zone 9)
- can grow to 7-10 feet in height
- be careful, this whole plant is poisonous so keep it away from young children and pets.

What it needs:
- lots of sun
- watering once a day
- feeding once a week
- bringing indoors in the winter

Scientific name:
Nerium oleander

Of course, oleander gives you that feeling of being in the Mediterranean. It has beautiful scented blossoms in white or yellow and every conceivable shade of pink and red, and dark green, pointed leaves.

You can buy oleander either as a small plant or one that is almost fully grown (it can grow to 7–10 feet in height), depending on your budget. It will withstand temperatures around freezing point but it is not hardy and must be brought indoors in areas where temperatures fall below freezing. Plant it in a pot so you can bring it inside in late fall and place it in a light airy spot (such as a garage or stairwell).

Oleander is a sun worshipper; the weather can't be too warm for this plant. So stand it in full sunlight, but water it daily and feed it once a week. It flowers from June through October. Remove any faded blooms regularly. Oleander doesn't take kindly to repotting, so it is best to put it in a really large container from the start.

The plant doctor warns: take care with small children and pets! All of this plant, from the flowers to the leaves, is poisonous.

Lavender

The butterflies and bees love it

What it is:
- small shrub with the unmistakable fragrance — of lavender!
- can last for 6-8 years ...
- ... and grow to 24–32 inches, or larger
- hardy (zone 5)
- silvery, needle-shaped leaves
- resistant to aphids, ants, and moths...
- ...but not to bees and butterflies!

What it needs:
- sunshine
- a sheltered spot
- clean soil
- plenty of room for the roots
- some frost protection in winter

Scientific name:
Lavandula angustifolia

It smells like ...yes, like... unmistakable, like lavender as a matter of fact! Or like a summer vacation in the south of France. On the Côte d'Azur there are endless vistas of lavender, a haze of purple-blue as far as the eye can see. So you can either settle there or plant some yourself!

Lavender is best bought as a young plant from March onward. It is not worth growing it yourself from seed. It needs a sunny spot protected from the wind, clean soil, and as much space as possible for the root system to expand. In return you will be rewarded with small purple-blue flowers from July through September.

Trim it from time to time, otherwise it will develop into a mini-hedge and quickly become woody except at the tips. In colder areas, cover it with spruce branches as frost protection during the winter.

What to plant with it:
Planted near or underneath roses, lavender will repel aphids and ants. Bunches of dried lavender make the ideal moth repellent in drawers and closets.

Tip:
Not only bees and butterflies have a taste for the fragrant blooms — so do humans. Try sprinkling candied lavender on desserts (for candying, see page 109).

Jasmine

A feast for the eyes and the nose

What it is:
- shrub bearing heavily perfumed white flowers from June through October
- not hardy (zone 7)
- together with lavender and oleander the ultimate combination of Mediterranean scents

What it needs:
- sunshine
- regular watering in summer
- feeding every two weeks
- bringing indoors in winter

Scientific name:
Jasminum officinale

It is late summer and you are vacationing in a small Greek seaside village. Siesta time is over and it's time to take yourself slowly (because of the heat!) down to the harbor for an ice-cold drink. Suddenly, you are almost knocked out by the strong scent of flowers from courtyards, patios, and balconies. Then you think, "Haven't I smelled that perfume somewhere before?" Jasmine is certainly no stranger.

Jasmine needs to be in a big container, in full sun. It needs regular watering and feeding every two weeks in summer.

In cold climates, move it into a bright, airy, cool location, such as a stairwell in winter, and water only occasionally. Jasmine sheds its leaves in winter, but don't panic, this is perfectly normal.

The plant doctor advises caution, however. The beguiling scent given off by the white flowers can cause severe headaches for some people.

Olive tree

As old as Methuselah and brimming with personality

What it is:
• evergreen tree with silvery, blue-green shimmering leaves
• produces flowers but no olives in cooler climates
• can withstand the cold ...
• ... but is not hardy (zone 8)

What it needs:
• full sun
• watering every 2 weeks
• feeding once a month
• bringing indoors in late fall

Scientific name:
Olea europaea

You can bring a little Mediterranean romance (goats under the olive tree, clear skies, the taste of salt on your lips) into your home with a genuine olive tree! For growing at home, the olive comes as a shrub or a small tree. The bigger the plant the more expensive it will be, since olive trees grow very slowly. That is why, in their native habitat, they can live to a biblical age — up to several hundred years.

In July and August the tree produces small, creamy-white bunches of flowers, but if you live in one of the cooler growing zones, the flowers will not bear fruit, so you will not have any olives.

The olive tree enjoys a sunny spot and needs to be watered every two weeks and fed about once a month.

Olive trees are tough and can survive temperatures around freezing point. Nevertheless, in cold climates they should be brought into a lighted stairwell or garage. The olive tree keeps its leaves over winter.

Repotting is best done in spring and pruning can be done at any time. And what's more, diseases are rare.

Tip:
Create peace with your olive. How? Present your dear friends (or enemies) with olive branches - a symbol of peace!

Lemon and Mandarin

A duo for the *dolce vita*

What they are:
• evergreen trees or shrubs
• redolent of the subtropics
• very sensitive to cold (zone 9)
• grow to 10 feet high
• leaves and flowers strongly perfumed

What they need:
• strong sunshine in a sheltered location
• regular watering
• preferably special soil
• feeding every two weeks
• must be brought indoors in the fall

Scientific names:
Citrus reticulata (mandarin) and *Citrus limon* (lemon)

Hard to believe, but true. Oranges and lemons don't grow in nets in supermarkets, but at home in pots! The little white flowers and the firm, dark green, oval leaves are heavily perfumed with the citrus scent.

There are many species of citrus. All are evergreen and have small white and/or pink flowers.

Buy bushy shrubs and plant them in pots (make sure the pots are not too small) or planters.

Citrus trees need a sunny, sheltered location. Water them regularly, or the leaves, as well as the lemons, will turn yellow. With regular feeding you may (perhaps) be lucky enough to get a crop....

They hate the frost, of course, so if you live in a colder climate, citrus trees must be brought into the house in the fall (preferably in a very cool, light and airy spot; a dark place will suffice but the plant will shed its leaves). Citrus do not take kindly to having waterlogged roots, so make sure the soil is well drained (pages 14–15).

The plant doctor warns that citrus varieties are not only attractive to humans but also to aphids, scale insects, and mealybugs.

What to plant with it:
Don't plant citrus near apple trees, as they will shed their leaves.

Fig tree

Haute couture à la Adam and Eve

What it is:
• tree with large, succulent green leaves
• flowers from April through June
• fruit will set if there is plenty of sunshine
• sheds its leaves in winter
• can overwinter in a dark corner of the house

What it needs:
• plenty of sunshine
• watering daily
• fertilizing once a week
• bringing indoors in winter (zone 7)

Scientific name:
Ficus carica

This attractive native of the Mediterranean has been around at least since the days of Adam and Eve. It grows into a magnificent tree and the distinctively shaped, large, flat leaves serve as "nature's umbrella."

In colder areas, buy fig trees in late spring (mid-May), when there is no longer any danger of ground frost, so they can be put outdoors immediately. By the way, fruit may set even in cooler growing zones if the summer happens to be particularly warm. It depends entirely on the weather. A wet summer means there will be no crop.

Fig trees enjoy sunny, warm locations but need watering daily and feeding once a week in summer.

In cool climates, bring it into the house to overwinter in a cool location. Since it loses its leaves it can be in a dark location.

Cooking Tip:
Don't worry if your fig tree doesn't bear fruit. Mission figs from the market taste very good too. Try fresh figs as an appetizer with wafer-thin slices of Parma or Smithfield ham. Or as a dessert with almond cookies and vanilla ice cream sprinkled with amaretto liqueur. The Greeks used fig tree branches for curdling milk to make cheese.

47

Agapanthus

A gardener's best friend!

What it is:
- evergreen perennial
- grows up to 40 inches tall
- strap-shaped leaves
- blue or white flower heads on long stems
- not hardy (zone 9)

What it needs:
- lots of water ...
- ... but no "wet feet"
- weekly feeding until the flowering season
- to be taken indoors in winter

Scientific name:
Agapanthus praecox

Perfect on any Mediterranean-style balcony, with its long leaves and luxuriant violet-blue or white flower heads on long straight stems (July/August).

Buy as a ready-grown young plant and put into the biggest pot available. Lilies do not like to be moved and do not take kindly to being transferred to another pot — the punishment: no flowers! The contrary is also true: the more pot-bound the lily becomes the more luxuriantly it blooms.

It needs a sunny spot with protection from the wind and plenty of water every day in the summer (but don't let it stand in water) and a weekly feed up till flowering time.

During winter in colder zones, bring it into a light stairwell and only water occasionally. In warmer areas leave it outside as long as it has protective covering. Beware: if it's too warm in winter nothing will come of the flowers!

It is seldom affected by pests or diseases.

Rock rose

Fashionable in England

What it is:
- evergreen shrub, growing 2 – 7 feet
- beautiful delicate red or white flowers, depending on the variety
- not hardy (zones 7–9)
- a favorite Mediterranean plant in English gardens

What it needs:
- sunshine
- regular watering
- feeding once a week
- bringing indoors in winter

Scientific name:
Cistus sp.

The rock rose, with its delicate, heavily scented flowers, is almost a "must" in English gardens . Since many parts of England and Scotland have a warm microclimate, the rock rose happily reveals itself in all its glory. The flowers are very impressive. Depending on the variety they may be white speckled with brown (*Cistus ladanifer*), white speckled with yellow (*C. laurifolius*), or pink with red-brown spots (*C. purpureus*).

Buy small specimens and plant them in pots or containers. If you live in a cold region, move them indoors in the fall.

Place in a warm, sunny location, water regularly, and feed weekly up to the middle of August. It is important to cut it back a little after flowering and only water sparingly when it is in its winter quarters (which should be light and airy).

Angel's trumpet

The diva of plants performs a solo

What it is:
• shrub or tree that grows to a height and width of about 10 feet
• has white, yellow, or pink trumpet-shaped flowers with a heady perfume
• extremely poisonous...
• ... but not hardy (zone 9)

What it needs:
• lots of water
• plenty of room
• fertilizing once a week
• spending the winter indoors

Scientific name:
Brugmansia spp.

Angels' trumpets have forceful personalities. They don't simply hang around looking noncommital, they are a real experience. This is partly due to the magnificent blooms that grow up to 12 inches long, to which they owe their common name, and which carry a heady perfume.

It is best to buy angel's trumpet as small plants and put them outside in pots from the end of May. A large pot is essential. The angel's trumpet can grow to a height of ten feet and be just as wide. It has sharp prickles. Flowering is from June through October.

It needs a warm location, though out of direct sunlight. It also needs plenty of water (it is best to water in the mornings and in the evenings). A weekly feed is essential.

In colder zones, treat this plant like an annual, or overwinter in a cool, light place. Specimens that have grown too big can be pruned back.

The plant doctor advises caution. The angel's trumpet, a South American native, is poisonous. Never put this plant near children or pets.

Bougainvillea

A high-living sun-worshipper

What it is:
• shrub that climbs over surrounding undergrowth
• fast-growing (10–13 feet tall)
• magnificent blooms, mainly purple
• very sensitive to the cold (zone 9)

What it needs:
• sunny, sheltered location
• moderate daily watering
• feeding once a week
• bringing indoors in early fall

Scientific name:
Bougainvillea

The bougainvillea is a true "wonder plant." It grows quickly into a sturdy shrub between 10 and 13 feet tall. In warm summers it flowers in such profusion that the whole plant is covered with purple, red, pink, white, or orange-yellow flowers, depending on the variety.

Bougainvillea loves warm, sunny locations protected from the wind. The more sunshine there is, the greater the profusion of flowers. In wet summers, this sun-worshipper saves its flowers for the following year. Bougainvillea is very sensitive to the cold and should be grown in pots in colder zones, if you want to overwinter it indoors.

Water regularly, especially when it is warm (long periods without water will cause it to shed leaves), and from April through August feed once a week. This climbing shrub needs some kind of support, but bear in mind that it should not be permanent. In the fall, prune heavily, and it will grow better the following season. Repot about every 2–3 years.

Bring bougainvillea inside to a cool, well-lit room before the first frost.

It is possible to propagate bougainvillea through cuttings (see pages 20–21), but this is not a job for a novice gardener.

European grapevine

Needs a south-facing balcony or slope

What it is:
- fast-growing perennial vine ...
- ... with attractive, large leaves
- can grow to 16 feet
- if there is plenty of sunshine you might get a grape harvest in September/October

What it needs:
- plenty of sun and a warm southern aspect
- daily watering
- a climbing support and winter protection (zone 6)

Scientific name:
Vitis vinifera

No respectable Greek verandah could manage without this shade-giving plant. You can create your own vine canopy at home. Buy established plants and put them out in late April through early May. For successful climbing plant them at a slight angle.

The vine is fast-growing, as long as the summer is not too wet. It needs a trellis, bamboo stakes, or a pergola to climb on. Tie the branches lightly to the structure.

Give it a sunny, sheltered location, preferably a south-facing house wall. Water daily from May through September, but only occasionally thereafter. Depending on your climatic zone and weather conditions, you may get a crop of black or green grapes, depending on the variety.

The vine is tough, and if covered with conifer branches it will generally survive both snow and ice. My own attempts at growing a vine against a wall in the mountains — in spite of the most severe weather conditions — are proof of this.

Pomegranate tree

Especially hot-blooded

What it is:
- densely branched tree or shrub
- grows up to 7 feet tall
- not hardy (zone 9)

What it needs:
- plenty of sun
- virtually no wind
- regular watering
- feeding every 1–2 weeks
- moving indoors in the fall

Scientific name:
Punica granatum

Top tip: the dwarf variety 'Nana' grows quickly, but only up to 40 inches high.

In cooler zones, the pomegranate is exclusively an ornamental tree. It will not bear fruit, due to too little sun, but it produces brilliant red flowers in late summer. The dwarf variety 'Nana' flowers virtually on the spot and in great profusion.

Sun and a sheltered location are absolutely necessary. Prune lightly in February/March for a bushier plant the following year.

As a hot-blooded Mediterranean plant, the pomegranate wants nothing to do with the cold, of course. Move it indoors to a light, cool place before the first night frost. Water occasionally while it is indoors.

Strawberry tree

The Mediterranean heather

What it is:
- evergreen shrub or small tree …
- … with strawberry-like fruit
- and flowers in winter
- not hardy but will withstand temperatures around freezing for a short time (zone 7)

What it needs:
- daily watering …
- … but don't let it get waterlogged
- feeding once a week
- bringing indoors in winter

Scientific name:
Arbutus unedo

The strawberry tree is a sort of Mediterranean heather, with elongated laurel-like leaves, flowers from November through March, and edible fruits that bear a slight resemblance to strawberries. In fact, they have a rather bland taste — but eating them is not the point, as strawberry trees are grown for their looks and they are very attractive plants.

The strawberry tree prefers bright light, though preferably not full sun, and protection from the wind. Water a little every day so the plant does not dry out, but don't let it get waterlogged. Feed once a week from May through September. You can trim it to shape, and it does not object to being repotted in spring.

The strawberry tree will tolerate a slight frost, but in cold zones, bring it indoors, into a cool, bright place in the fall.

Dwarf palm

To help create your own boardwalk atmosphere

What it is:
- not too sensitive to the cold…
- …but not hardy in colder regions (zone 9)
- very bushy, with fan-shaped, deeply-serrated leaves
- … but slow-growing

What it needs:
- full sun to shady locations
- regular watering
- feeding every two weeks
- wintering indoors

Scientific name:
Chamaerops humilis

Palm trees are the symbol of summer, sun, and sea. As soon as the first palm appears on the journey southward, you know you are really there! For the imported Mediterranean or Floridian effect, at least one palm tree is a must! The dwarf palm is just the thing for your private boardwalk. It is not too sensitive to the cold and is grown as an ornamental in northern Europe. It will not grow more than 7 feet tall, and it grows slowly. The leaves are sharp and thorny and it's easy to prick yourself, so keep it away from children.

The dwarf palm likes to live in a bright, sunny spot but will also thrive in shady locations. In summer, it needs plenty of water every day and feeding every two weeks. Take care to water the soil, not into the hollow of the leaf, or you may rot the leaf.

The dwarf palm won't collapse with shock at the first sign of cold, but in colder zones, bring it indoors, into a cool, well-lit location, and water occasionally.

The plant doctor warns that if the dwarf palm is kept too warm in winter it will be attacked by aphids and scale insects.

Thyme

Strongly aromatic

What it is:
• small shrub, grows up to 12 inches tall
• strong, aromatic scent, small leaves, and lilac through pink flowers
• some varieties are hardier than others (zones 5–7)

What it needs:
• plenty of sun
• occasional feeding

Scientific name:
Thymus vulgaris

Thyme smells aromatic and has a bitter taste. It can grow to 12 inches tall. The woody stems bear tender shoots with small green leaves.

It is best to buy thyme already growing in pots. When buying plants, check the hardiness. Some varieties are a good choice in colder zones because they tolerate snow and ice. Some are mostly ornamental; the one that's generally used as a herb in cooking is *T. vulgaris*. Try the specialty thymes, such as orange and lemon thyme.

Thyme has few soil requirements; it even grows in the crevices of cliffs and walls. It demands strong sunlight, fast-draining soil, and feeding (preferably with an organic fertilizer) every three months. It can definitely do without too much rain and soggy conditions. Water sparingly. In May and June it shows off its pinkish-lilac flowers.

What grows with it:
Plant thyme near potatoes or tomatoes — it is said to promote growth in both.

Cooking Tip:

For cooking, use the shoots with the smallest leaves. The flowers taste delicious in a summer salad. Thyme pairs well with tomato dishes.

Sage

A classic with poultry and pork dishes

What it is:
• small shrub that grows to a height of about 2 to 3 feet
• hardy even in very cold zones if well covered (zone 5)

What it needs:
• sun
• very little water and even less plant food
• well-drained soil

Scientific name:
Salvia officinalis

Sage is a strongly flavored herb that is added to rich meat and vegetable dishes. It is an essential ingredient in the Italian dish Saltimbocca alla Romana, a small veal cutlet topped with a slice of Parma ham and a sage leaf and fried.

Sage can grow up to 3 feet tall and has woody branches bearing many sprigs. The long oval leaves are silvery gray and velvety to the touch. When rubbed between the fingers, they give off a pleasant fragrance.

Buy sage plants in the spring and plant in a sheltered, very sunny spot (although it will also do fine in semishade). It doesn't matter too much if you forget to water and you don't need to worry about feeding it in most soils. The attractive bluish-violet flowers last from June through August.

Sage can tolerate harsh winters if covered with spruce branches and some straw. Cut the plant back by about a third in spring, and it will put out strong new growth.

Rosemary

Evergreen, always tasty, and delicious with lamb

What it is:
- evergreen shrub...
- ...but not hardy (zones 8–10)
- woody stems with needle-shaped leaves
- aromatic scent, not unlike pine, and a strong resinous taste

What it needs:
- full sun
- too dry rather than too wet conditions
- feeding once per season
- bringing indoors in winter

Scientific name:
Rosmarinus officinalis

This evergreen shrub can grow up to six feet in favorable conditions. As with sage and thyme, buy plants in the spring. Rosemary is not hardy in cooler zones (borderline zones can try mulching it over winter). It's best to grow it in a container and bring it indoors when it gets very cold. Overwinter in a well-lit, frost-free location. It can come out again in mid-May.

Just like all the lucky plants that are native to the Mediterranean, rosemary is used to a great deal of sunshine. It doesn't like soil that is too damp and it needs excellent drainage. From April through June it has small, pale blue flowers, similar to those of sage and thyme. Ideal as a salad garnish.

Cooking Tip:

Add small sprigs of rosemary to lamb, poultry, and vegetable dishes — it gives an instant flavor of the Mediterranean. Chop it finely and rub or sprinkle it over meat.

Bay tree

Caesar himself was conquered by its fragrance

What it is:
- evergreen tree or shrub with leathery, aromatic leaves
- the leaves have many uses in cooking (and don't forget the victor's laurel wreath)

What it needs:
- sunshine
- watering regularly
- feeding once a week
- bringing indoors in winter (zone 8)

Scientific name:
Laurus nobilis

At last we can pick our own bay leaves!

Bay trees have elongated, shiny leaves with an aromatic, slightly bitter scent. That's all they have in a cold climate, but in the South they also have flowers and berries. Bay trees are usually sold as container plants with a long trunk with a rounded crown.

Bay trees are sun-lovers (of course) but also thrive in shady locations. They need watering regularly (they must never be allowed to dry out) and feeding once a week. Bay trees are not over-sensitive, however. They can stand drastic pruning (even topiary work) and will tolerate a certain amount of cold. In cooler zones, bring them into a cool, light location before the first frosts.

The plant doctor warns that bay trees are prone to scale insects.

For a Special Party

Happenings

For a scintillating garden party, try story-telling, fire-eating, snake-charming, dressing up as famous people, quick sketch artists, Indian magicians, whip-cracking fortune tellers, or singing groups (find them through an entertainment agency, student employment register, or the want ads). Or entertain yourselves with a hilarious outdoor karaoke session.

Say cheese!

Play party-casting with Polaroids. Take a photograph of everyone right from the first arrival. Hang the guests' pictures on a line stretched across the garden, holding them in place with clothespins. Then through the haze of the following day, everyone can see what they looked like only a few hours before, when they were still fresh and bright-eyed.

Cheesy!

Or why not try looking like Arnold Schwarzenegger for a change? Make a color photocopy of Arnold cut out from a magazine and enlarged to life size. Stick it on cardboard and cut a hole where the face is. The guests put their heads through the opening and have themselves photographed with an instant camera, so everyone can share the joke.

From the grill I'll eat my fill

Once you try it, you'll be hooked forever. Serve everything wrapped in banana leaves (obtainable from Asian stores). Whether it's fish, meat, or vegetables , the food stays lovely and moist in its natural package. Or use lemongrass twigs, peeled and sharpened, instead of wooden or metal skewers.

Hip dips

....are the ideal accompaniments to grilled foods. Try Indonesian sambal oelek with apricot jam, lime juice, and red chili pepper rings. Or Indian chutney with yogurt, cumin, cayenne pepper, and fresh coriander. Or Mediterranean tapenade with minced black olives, capers, and anchovies, seasoned with balsamic vinegar, olive oil, and chili powder.

Enlightenment

.... guaranteed. For example, with candles (for outdoor use). Or flaming torches or candle lanterns. Chinese lanterns are festive, but keep a bucket of water handy as they are made of paper.

Irresistible!

Candlelight can not only be atmospheric and hugely romantic, but it also has other uses—as a mosquito repellent for instance. These candles are available in attractive, tiny, terra-cotta pots from garden centers, drugstores, and hardware stores. They drive away the most vicious guests, but the nice ones stay behind.

Fortune cookies

People at parties can run out of small talk. You can liven things up by passing out fortune cookies. The messages usually say nice things like "Fate knows and is kind" or "Glamor will enter your life this week." You can buy them at Chinese stores, or order them via the Internet (www.excite.com).

Spring rolls

Soften some rice paper (obtainable from Asian groceries) in cold water and drain on paper towels. Lay Asian mint, Thai basil leaves, shredded pak choi, and Chinese cabbage on the rice papers and fold them into packages. Serve with hoisin sauce. Unusual and authentic!

Homemade potato chips

Slice washed, unpeeled new potatoes lengthwise in fairly thick slices. Cover a cookie sheet with nonstick baking paper and arrange the slices on it. Mix olive oil with chili powder and salt, brush the mixture over the potatoes, and bake until crisp in a preheated 400°F oven for 30–40 minutes. Serve with various dips.

Refreshing!

Here are two fresh, alcohol-free ideas. Purée honeydew melon flesh, sprinkle with lime juice, pour ice-cold sparkling mineral water over it, and serve on crushed ice. And this pick-me-up will brighten the spirits of tired guests: blend avocado with yogurt, add one teaspoon of wheat germ per person, stir, and season with salt, Tabasco, and lime juice. Instant energy!

Turbo

Patience is a virtue, but it won't get you far!

Green

It's March, then April — it's May already! Yet on the third-floor balcony of the apartment just above us, nothing is happening at all. The whole place is bare. Plastic flowerpots painted in camouflage colors are lying around without much to fill them. This is not news — they've always done it this way.

Then, all of a sudden, surprise, surprise! There is a sudden explosion on all sides. From empty flowerpots to massed greenery. From zero to green in one week. This is also the way they do it.

Let's ask our neighbors, experts in the fastest-growing balcony garden in the city, how they do it. They don't just dabble, they are into turbo-growth big-time. They buy lots of young scarlet runner beans and pack them tightly into pots. In two to three weeks the beans burst forth in a riot of greenery, followed by brilliant red flowers.

So that's what I am going to do, too.

Styling Tip
The sleeping beauty and the bank clerk

To our left, the enormously attractive back wall of our neighbor's garage, to our right a balcony just as breathtakingly ugly with its empty beer cases, a step-ladder, and a broken plastic chair. Ugh! This is a case for the Sleeping Beauty Project.

First step: plant a turbo-climber in a large tub in each balcony corner (scarlet runner bean, morning glory, hop, or something like that — see the following pages).

Second step: install a spider's web of bamboo canes and string for the plants to climb.

Third step: collect more planters and tubs and fill them with as many vigorously growing plants as possible. The Sleeping Beauty can now rest in her castle, surrounded by the impenetrable hedge. It is time for the handsome prince to come and rescue her (though it might be the clerk from the bank around the corner, instead).

Five times as fast
Quick gardens for quick gardeners!

In these fast-moving times – that's a bad start to any sentence, and it will probably get worse. "Fast" and "quick" are words that are associated with a stressful and hectic lifestyle. But is that always the case? People who act fast are quick-thinking, they have character, a zest for life, and a desire to see plenty of action in the garden. These people will love the turbo-plants in this chapter, because they speed up the growing process. Perhaps they'll do one of the following:
1. Quick parties: a fast person likes to host impromptu parties, theme parties, such as Italian with Parma ham, melon, and grissini (breadsticks). Or French with a French stick, cheese, and red wine.
2. Quick changes: a quick person is flexible and likes to make lots of changes. This person would rather not plan his/her garden to last for an eternity. For him/her, annuals are the most suitable plants. I change, so my garden should be allowed to change too.
3. Fast enjoyment. Such a person takes advantage of an opportunity. "If the sun is shining now, sit in my garden for quarter of an hour and recharge my batteries. After all, who knows what the weather will be tomorrow."
4. Fast alterations. A fast person is pragmatic and can live with the fact that his/her balcony has not been fully renovated, and does as the Greeks do, that is, paint old walls white.
5. Fast shoes. A fast person can't change into or out of awkward gardening shoes every time he/she goes into or out of the house. So get some rubber thongs that are easy to slip in and out of.

The ideal way to a balcony lawn

Garden centers are often located out of town (cars, traffic jams, long lines at the checkout counter). But the town gardener takes advantage of other stores that might stock gardening stuff.

Pet stores, for instance, have sand for the soil-sand mix that many plants, such as lupins, need. What's more, it's sold in easy-to-manage small bags, instead of the huge heavy quantities you tend to find in a garden center.

Catgrass is a trendsetter among turbo-plants. Plant the seeds evenly and not too deeply in the soil. Keep watering generously (other demands: none), and before you can say Jack Robinson, the strong dark stalks will shoot out of the ground, up to 20 inches high. Catgrass is an annual, it dies in fall, and is no more.

Dogs and cats like to nibble on it, and we like it, because it looks attractive, the ideal way to create a balcony lawn. Plant it as a border or as a sun screen in tubs with other plants. Or, if you like, plant a whole pot or flower-box full of it. It grows incredibly fast, is easy to tend, and is decorative and inexpensive.

The story of S.

This story doesn't have a very romantic beginning to it (lonely and all by herself, she waited in a bag on the seed shelf of a garden center), and furthermore, it continues underground (in a seed tray on the window sill). The heroine, however, then struggles out of the darkness into the light at a dramatic speed (in 8 to 10 days) and develops (like Phoenix out of potting mixture) into a real Hollywood star (growing to more than two feet in height).

Diary

After such an exciting trailer, we present, for the first time, exclusive extracts from the diary of S.

April 1
Done it! A Basic Gardener picked me up and packed me into seed-trays. Then I was placed on a sunny window sill in a well-heated room. I feel that I am given water regularly but not too much, and that I'm moving toward fulfilling my true destiny.

April 10
It's a breakthrough — hooray, the light of day at last! I'm probably still looking a bit crushed. But if I continue to be watered, and get more sun and, if possible, no drafts, perhaps everything will turn out okay after all.

April 30
My Basic Gardener has to decide now. Will he choose the hard road and put me outdoors? It's good to be toughened up so that I can become hardy, and a little cold weather never harmed anybody. Or will he choose the soft option — first into larger pots, then continue to keep me warm and sheltered on the window sill?

May 15 - 30
Nothing can stop me now! Flower-boxes get ready — here I come!

June 15 - 30
That fertilizer was a real treat! I have surpassed myself. Without a broom handle there'd be no holding me.

July 30
I feel the end is near...was that it...bury my heart at Wounded Knee... my last wish.

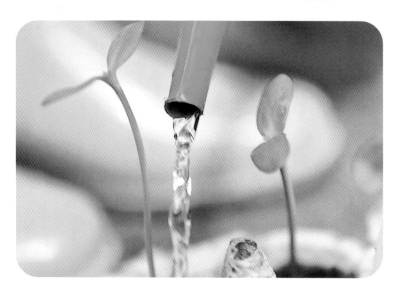

Morning glory

It's such an individual

What it is:
- annual climber, up to 8 feet
- blue or red flowers
- blooms from July through October

What it needs:
- plenty of water
- feeding once a week
- no rain or wind
- climbing support

Scientific name:
Ipomoea tricolor

Closed in the afternoons! The blue or red funnel-shaped flowers only open in the mornings. So please don't arrive too late to admire the morning glory. It certainly punishes the sleepyhead, the late riser, does morning glory.

Start morning glory from seed in March or April, and replant the seedlings individually in pots. From mid-May, they can be put into their final location, which should be well protected. Plant them around 16 inches apart. Since it is a strong climber, morning glory needs vertical rods, wires, or strings for climbing.

Morning glory always needs generous watering, but hates wind and rain. Fertilize it weekly. Some morning glory are perennials. Others die after flowering, living for only one summer.

The plant doctor warns that morning glory seeds are poisonous, so keep them out of reach of children.

Styling Tip:
Put pots of various climbers together; morning glory with Black-eyed Susan (page 76) is an especially attractive combination.

Creeping zinnia

Miniature sunflower with maximum appeal

What it is:
• a hardy annual ...
• yellow flowers bloom from June through October

What it needs:
• nothing but sunshine

Scientific name:
Sanvitalia procumbens

Not much care — that's what we like. You can sow creeping zinnia from March onward. Sow it in a miniature greenhouse or indoors, because it likes growing in pleasant room temperatures. If you buy it, wait until mid-May before planting out the young zinnias. Plant them about 6 inches apart.

Creeping zinnia appreciates permeable soil, so mix the soil with about one-third sand. Apart from that, it hardly asks for anything. Watering is rarely necessary, and it only needs a little fertilizing once a month. If you dead-head the withered flowers, it will flower, and flower, and flower... right into the fall. Throw it away after that; it only lives for one summer.

Sunflower

The sunny side of the street

What it is:
• an annual that grows up to 10 feet high
• flowers in early and midsummer
• has large, bright yellow flowers

What it needs:
• full sunshine and warmth
• lots of water and feeding
• no waterlogged ground and no wind

Scientific name:
Helianthus annuus

Sunflowers are the perfect choice for all those impatient gardeners. Sunflowers grow from zero to up to 10 feet in a matter of months! Even miniature varieties such as 'Teddy Bear' manage to grow to almost three feet.

Grow them from seed, planting one seed per pot in late March-April, or buy young plants in early summer. Replant 8 inches apart. And then watch it grow — and don't twist your neck while doing so.

It wants everything, this sunflower, and plenty of it: sun, warmth, and water. But it's allergic to waterlogged soil. Fertilize once a week until August. Normal soil is perfectly adequate. For an optimum effect, the soil in the flower bed should have a little sand mixed in with it, but that's not absolutely necessary. Considering its height, the sunflower does have a fantastic sense of balance, but at some time or another, it will need a strong shoulder to lean on (a bamboo stick will do the trick).

The plant doctor warns that Sclerotina disease, a fungus, can attack sunflowers. Cut off and burn rotting, discolored stalks, as they are infectious.

Styling Tip:
For a non-stop sunflower show of sunny yellow blooms all through the summer:
- plant the seeds in March for flowers in early summer
- buy young plants in May for flowers in summer
- buy young plants in the summer for flowers in the fall

Wisteria

Romantic — but make it snappy!

What it is:
• very fast-growing perennial climber (zone 5)
• grows up to 50 feet
• a cascade of blue flowers from April through May

What it needs:
• a sunny, sheltered location
• sufficient water
• lime-free fertilizer in spring
• a firm climbing support
• winter protection if grown in a tub in cooler climates

Scientific name:
Wisteria sinensis

Wisteria makes a most attractive cover for house walls, pergolas, garages, or any unsightly buildings. It has attractively shaped leaves, long tendrils, and cascades of 12-inch-long blue flowers.

Buy and plant wisteria in spring. If planting in the garden, fertilize the soil if in a container, use normal potting mixture. You will need a really big container, around 20 inches high and 20 inches in diameter, because wisteria has a strong root system. You will need to aggressively prune wisteria, especially in a container. Even in the garden, a wisteria plant will crush an irritating drain-pipe or gutter that gets in its way. It needs a very sturdy climbing support, along which you can direct it with thick wire to make it grow where you want it. Its stem quickly becomes woody, so that it cannot be trained when it is older.

In very dry weather, wisteria needs plenty of water. In spring, it needs a little lime-free fertilizer (page 25). It doesn't flower for the first two or three years, but when it does, the flowers are spectacular cascades of violet-blue clusters. Prune thoroughly after flowering. If it's in a pot, it can stay outdoors in winter, but wrap it up warmly. Wisteria sheds its leaves in winter.

Nasturtium

No fence could be that pretty

What it is:
• annual climber with shoots up to 10 feet long
• definitely the prettiest and least expensive method to make a fence disappear
• flowers from May through October...
• ...in fiery colors

What it needs:
• plenty of sunshine
• daily watering
• a climbing support

Scientific name:
Tropaeolum majus

It's not surprising the nasturtium is so popular. It is strikingly attractive, with large, velvety flowers in yellow, orange, and scarlet, and pretty, circular leaves.

Plant the seeds straight into flowerpots or borders in late April. You only need to start seeds indoors if you are living in a really cold growing zone. The previous year's seed will germinate where it falls, showing it was happy with the location in which you planted it.

Nasturtium prefers a sunny site and nutrient-rich soil. A wire fence is an ideal climbing support, as the tendrils easily wrap around the thin wires. It soon becomes invisible under a colorful flower screen. Water this plant daily but do not feed it.

Notwithstanding its perfection, the plant doc cannot conceal the fact that nasturtium has a weakness. Its beauty attracts not only human beings but aphids as well.

Cup-and-saucer vine

The five-minute jungle

What it is:
• vigorous climber
• usually only lives for one summer
• even in a tub it grows 10–16 feet
• violet flowers from July through to frost

What it needs:
• plenty of sunshine and water
• feeding every two weeks
• climbing support

Scientific name:
Cobaea scandens

Cup-and-saucer vine is a late developer. It doesn't really start growing and flowering until July. But when it takes off, it *really* takes off. By the end of the summer, you could have a screen that's 14 feet high! And that's in a tub on your balcony or patio.

Sow the seed on your window sill from February onward. Prick out the seedlings in March, 28 inches apart. It likes living in flowerbeds and borders, but grows just as fast in tubs, though they must be large ones.

Give this vine a good strong climbing support. The plant has feathery leaves and a mass of bell-shaped flowers, green at first, then turning violet, though you can also get it in white.

Give it plenty of water and fertilizer every two weeks. If you want it to branch out, instead of doggedly heading toward the top, keep nipping off the tips of the shoots (page 26).

Cup-and-saucer vine is usually grown as an annual because overwintering is difficult, but if you would like to try it, provide a cool, bright location.

Balloon vine

Truly weird

What it is:
• annual climber with tendrils up to 10 feet long…
• …and unusual, balloon-shaped fruit

What it needs:
• plenty of sunshine
• lots of water and fertilizer
• climbing support

Scientific name:
Cardiospermum

The leaves of this vine are reminiscent of grape leaves. In no time, they will have covered everything with greenery, but its very special characteristic are the yellow flowers that look like small, fat, captive balloons.

The balloon vine needs a lot of warmth (around 77°F) in order to germinate. In cooler zones, wait until May, and buy balloon vine seedlings. Plant them about 20 inches apart.

The balloon vine insists on a sunny, sheltered position and climbing support right from the beginning. And it needs plenty of water and fertilizer, preferably every 2–4 weeks.

It's not that difficult to grow vegetables for ourselves. Vegetables like zucchini and cucumbers are not just appreciated for their nutritional values and flavor. No, we love them for their attractive appearance and their climbing qualities. They are truly magnificent plants that produce bright green leaves and attractive curling tendrils in no time at all.

Zucchini

Divine vine

What it is:
- a type of squash...
- ...that looks like a cucumber
- yellow flowers...
- ...and huge, decorative leaves
- easy to grow

What it needs:
- lots of sunshine, water, and space

Scientific name:
Cucurbita pepo

Aside from being edible, we think zucchini is really beautiful, with its star-shaped, golden blossoms and wide-spreading leaves. A prima donna among the squash! And a wonderful item for your instant jungle.

Plant the seeds in pots or a cold frame (two seeds per pot; remove the smaller one later). Lazy-bones can buy young plants in early summer at the garden center. Two plants are more than enough for a balcony or patio. In mid to late May, the young zucchini can be moved, either into the garden (plant them wide apart; leave at least 32 inches between them) or into a very large tub.

Zucchini always wants to be pleasantly moist, especially in dry weather, but don't let water get on the flowers. Fertilize container plants once a week, and give those in the garden a smaller dose every 3 to 4 weeks.

Harvest about 8–10 weeks after sowing (depending on the variety).

What to plant with it:
Zucchini gets on well with runner beans and nasturtiums.

Hop

Not in beer for a change

What it is:
- annual turbo-screen
- grows up to 14 feet
- does not mind a northern aspect

What it needs:
- sun to partial shade
- a climbing support is a must
- plenty of water but good drainage
- fertilizing every two months
- no rain or wind

Scientific name:
Humulus lupulus

This herbaceous perennial is best known as an ingredient in beer. The white flowers are not really important. Although they are quite pretty, they are small and inconspicuous. The point about the hop vine is that it covers everything with its elegant leaves on long stalks and does so in record time, only a few weeks after it has been planted. It doesn't even mind a northern aspect, which makes hop a candidate for a Basic Gardening award for being a tough guy.

Plant the seeds indoors in early March, then transfer the seedlings separately to pots. From mid-May onward, when the hop plant is big enough and the weather is warm enough, take the pots outdoors and replant into tubs or about 20 inches apart in beds. Hop will tolerate partial shade, but sun is better. Don't forget to give it a sturdy climbing support.

While the hop plant is growing, provide lots of water, but never let it get waterlogged. Fertilize every two months.

Hop flowers in July-August. After that, it's onto the compost heap with it!

Cucumber

A lot more attractive than its image

What it is:
- a lush and vigorous annual climber
- ...with yellow flowers
- ...a low-calorie, healthy fruit

What it needs:
- lots of warmth
- a lot of moisture and space
- a climbing support

Scientific name:
Cucumis sativus

Fancy a cucumber salad? Or home-made pickles? You can have them both with a homegrown cucumber plant, and it will look very pretty with its ornate tendrils and yellow flowers.

Sow it outdoors when the ground is thoroughly warm, or earlier on a warm window sill. Plant 3–4 seeds every 8 inches. Don't plant it outdoors in cool growing zones before mid May.

After the seedlings emerge, cut out the weakest and plant the strongest 16 inches apart. When they have five leaves, nip off the tips of the young plants, as this will give you many side shoots (page 26). The cucumber needs a sunny, sheltered location. If it grows too vigorously, you can prune the shoots (down to two leaves above the highest hanging cucumber fruit).

Keep the plant moist and always water it with pleasantly warm water. If the plant doesn't get enough water, the fruit will be bitter. It needs good drainage, however. Quite demanding, this cucumber, but we town gardeners will be able to make our own pickles from early July through September.

Scarlet runner bean

The fastest bean in town!

What it is:
- creates a thick, green curtain of foliage
- with curling tendrils...
- ...and fiery red, butterfly-shaped flowers from June through September
- a hardy annual

What it needs:
- never to be allowed to dry out
- not to be too hot
- fertilizing once a week

Scientific name:
Phaseolus coccineus

The scarlet runner bean is indeed a super-fast grower. It has large, deep green leaves with many scarlet flowers, so it's not surprising that one variety is known as 'Scarlet Emperor'.

Impatient gardeners who are in a rush to see this imperial splendor should plant the seeds indoors as early as mid-April. From mid-May you can plant them outside, leaving three inches between seeds. Runner beans like bright to partial shade and good ventilation. It soon needs something to hold on to, which is not surprising, considering it climbs to a height of eight feet. Make a climbing frame with string or wire. The plants flower from June through September, producing long, juicy beans that should be picked young, as the beans taste better and the plant will flower for longer.

To help prevent fungus disease and insect pests, the plant doctor suggests planting savory below the runners.

65

Class

Everything that has always been beautiful and truly basic

i c

Picture vivid red poppies and summer's sky-blue cornflowers by the
wayside: this is a classic. So is plum-colored columbine in meadows,
and pink traveler's joy turning in the fall to fluffy old-man's-beard along
a fence. Everything growing wild is a classic.

Lupines are also a classic, and sweet-smelling lilac, and delphiniums.
And so is the apple tree! Especially the apple tree. Tulips and daffodils in
spring are a classic, and mallow, and sweet peas, and lilies in summer.
And as for roses...Well, there's nothing more to be said.

Classics are European plants lovingly introduced into North American
colonies by homesick settlers. Classics are colorful, healthy, and robust.
And they flourish without a hothouse.

Above all, classic is anything we have always found to be beautiful.

Rose Basics

Roses really are true classics. Even if you aren't retired or an English aristocrat, you'll get along with them just fine.

There are thousands of different kinds of roses to suit every taste, from wild ones to delicate old garden roses to hybrid teas with star quality. And they come in every level of difficulty, from basic to manageable to real spoiled brats. And, of course, you can also get roses for your balcony. If you choose the right kind, roses really aren't difficult at all, as long as you remember a few Basic points.

Savvy shopping: when buying roses, look for those that are resistant to fungus diseases. Ask at your local garden center for roses that do well in your particular climate conditions. There are diseases that have specially adapted themselves to roses, such as powdery mildew (pages 28–29), black spot, and rust.

Proper planting: don't plant roses where roses have been planted before. This is because when the remains of the roots decay they emit substances that weaken their successors; this is often the case even when the soil has been completely changed.

Proper pruning: always dead-head roses, right down to , and including, the second strong leaf, to ensure repeat-blooming. For more tips on pruning, visit your local garden center.

The Flower Doctor Is On Call

What really works (or might work) on black spot, rust, etc.

Rusty brown or reddish spots on the leaves indicate the presence of rust fungus. Cut off affected parts of the plant immediately. Water only at the roots, not on the leaves; the rust fungus likes damp.

If there are round, dark brown or black spots on the leaves, and the leaves turn yellow and fall off, the rose has black spot, a fungus that attacks roses especially in rainy or cool weather. To help prevent black spot, make sure your roses have enough sun and space. You can try planting garlic between them. Remove all affected leaves and do not leave them lying around, as the fungus can survive the winter and return!

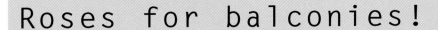

Roses for balconies!

You don't need your own private park to grow roses. A balcony is quite sufficient. Some miniature roses can be grown in pots very successfully.

You can find almost any type of rose from floribunda to tea roses as miniatures. These plants grow to a height of 10 to 20 inches. They require the same care and conditions as regular sized roses.

Some pretty hybrids you can try are:
• 'Baby Darling' — orange-pink double blooms
• 'Cinderella' — double pink and thornless
• 'Lemon Delight' — semidouble, clear yellow

Fruit tree Basics

A cottage, a garden, an apple tree — this is a classic combination...

Savvy shopping: only buy fruit trees from recognized mail order suppliers or garden centers, to make sure that the variety and size information are really accurate. Be sure to ask for rootstock that is suited to your growing zone and location. Miniature versions are created by grafting (attaching shoot of one tree to a relative with less vigorous growth).

An essential point, if you want fruit for most types of trees: always buy a partner for your fruit tree (ask at the garden center which is the right one) and plant them near each other. Otherwise, you will get no crop, because fruit trees only bear fruit if different varieties are planted together (this is known as "cross-fertilization"). However, if your neighbor happens to have a fruit tree, ask the name of the variety and get one to match and they will cross-fertilize each other. Fruit trees that don't need a partner include prune plum.

Proper planting: it's best to plant fruit trees in the fall. For miniature trees in pots, a 2½-gallon container filled with standard potting mix will be suitable at first. Later you will need one twice the size. In the garden, the distance between trees should be a little greater than the size to which the crown of the tree will grow. A very important point when planting miniature trees in the garden: the grafting point on the trunk must remain above ground. Otherwise, it will produce new roots and the tree will grow much larger than you want.

Proper pruning: a tree needs light and air to stay healthy, and proper pruning is the best way to ensure this. Unfortunately, this is not so Basic. We advise taking a course, such as those run by many gardening clubs in the spring. It's fun, it doesn't take a lot of time and then you have years to practice.

Fruit trees for balconies!

You don't need a city backyard to enjoy fruit trees and fruit. A balcony is quite enough. These hardy, miniature varieties of fruit tree will thrive even on the third floor.

Single-stem
Very narrow, no side shoots, and with a maximum height of 8 feet, it even fits on the balcony. You can pick fruit right from the tree (in high summer). Often after only one year, you'll get a hundred apples or more. Single-stem trees include apple, pear, plum, mirabelle, and morello cherry varieties. Protect well from frost in the winter.

Dwarf bush
Another specially bred miniature, maximum height 2.5 m, spreads out more than the single-stem form, but it's hardier (pages 80–81).

Hey there, pellitory!

The names of wild flowers have been handed down from ancient times and are sometimes quite rude-sounding. You could almost use them as insults, as in, "Hey there, pellitory! You old fat hen you! Hello, common sneezewort, how're you doing?" There are lots of plants associated with the devil, such as devil's bit scabious, so-called because the root looks as if part of it had been bitten off — probably by the devil. A more charming name is Himalayan balsam, originating in the Himalayas and now growing wild along the banks of streams. Or there is sundew, one of the few European carnivorous plants.

Born to be wild

Wild flowers grow all by themselves and all over the place. They are so beautiful, they could become a hobby. Our advice for boring Sundays is to take a wild flower guide and go for a walk, trying to recognize the plants. But do not dig them up. Many are protected. The enjoyment is in the knowledge rather than in possession.

Nice and relaxed

The cottage garden is a classic garden. Of course, the kitchen garden is of prime importance, with its beans, carrots, and peas, but that isn't the whole story. In the cottage garden, there is something of everything, whether it's edible or just good to look at, all growing together. Beds are framed by white and yellow stonecrop, zucchini grow with nasturtiums, cucumbers, and beans, and there are sunflowers, roses, wallflowers, lupines, delphiniums, stock, and mallows — anything goes! And it goes particularly well, because the secret of the cottage garden is that plants are put together to support one another; sunflowers and cucumbers, for instance (sunflowers and potatoes don't get on at all), plants that keep each other free of pests and disease, and plants that encourage each other in growth, blossom, and fruit.

Geranium

A wealth of blooms for beginners — very Basic

What it is:
• a hardy, weather-resistant perennial
• nice and traditional and really colorful
• blooms from April through October

What it needs:
• sun to semishade
• lots of moisture ...
• ... but no waterlogging
• to be indoors in winter (zone 10)

Scientific name:
Pelargonium peltatum

The geranium is simple, countrified, colorful, and fresh. Its personality makes it ideal casting for the lead part in a country farce. There are people who find it too conventional; we think it is nice and conventional, however. It all depends on where it's grown and how (and by whom). Geraniums will get a new look every time if, instead of planting them in great hordes, you set them as a single point of color; for example, in a plain terra-cotta pot. Their glowing flowers, ranging from white to pink, purple to blazing red, are the reason for their popularity — they look real impressive. They need very little work and they're decidedly weather-resistant.

Geraniums (their correct name is "pelargoniums") come in hanging varieties for hanging baskets or upright ones for flower beds. There are also scented varieties (page 84).

Plant your store-bought or home-grown plants (you can get more by making cuttings, pages 20–21) in the flower bed (8 inches apart) or in a pot. Water frequently at first, but be careful not to saturate them. Feed them once a week until the end of August and remove dead flowers.

For the winter, shorten long shoots and cut off all dead leaves and flowers. It is important not to move geraniums to their winter quarters if the roots are wet, so stop watering them well beforehand. In the winter, they need a light, cool, frost-free location and just a little water. Prune thoroughly in February (down to three or four lumps on the stem) and then put them into fresh soil.

A warning from the plant doctor: if the leaves wilt prematurely, the patient is suffering from black root rot and belongs in the trash, as there is a great danger of infection for other plants.

Lupine

A summer daydream

What it is:
- a decorative perennial
- grows to 3–4 feet
- flowers from June through August …
- …in many beautiful colors
- tenacious and hardy (zone 3)

What it needs:
- sun or semishade
- well-drained, sandy soil
- a little care

Scientific name:
Lupinus polyphyllus hybrids

They like to gather in large crowds, in white, yellow, pink, orange, red, blue, purple, or in two colors. They are reminiscent of everything to do with summer: summer vacations, summer light, summer love, summer scents…

Lupines make a great impression as they grow so tall, especially when planted as a brilliantly colorful backdrop in a bed behind shorter flowers. There are shorter varieties, however, that are compatible with balcony pots and grow to only two feet.

Sow lupines from April through July, 20 inches apart, right where they are to flower, or in pots. Remember, if you want them to amount to anything, lupines don't like soil that is too moist or too rich — they prefer it sandy and well-drained. In early fall, plant out the young plants, but please be careful; the roots don't like being transplanted. To compensate, you won't have to worry about them in the winter. Lupines can manage the winter without our help. In the following spring, add a little compost, but no mineral fertilizer.

Lupines flower from June through July. Afterward, it does them good to have the main shoots trimmed back except for more recent growth on the sides. Don't touch the leaves.

Larkspur

Truly idyllic

What it is:
- tenacious, hardy perennial (zones 3–9)
- grows up to 7 feet
- has glowing dark blue, delicate violet, or white flowers …
- …in June and July …
- …and again in September

What it needs:
- sunshine
- rich soil
- plenty of water during dry weather …
- …but no waterlogging

Scientific name:
Delphinium spp. (also the alternative common name)

The candle-shaped shimmering blue flower spikes grow 16 inches tall. There are many types and varieties. Garden hybrids are often labeled in garden centers as *Delphinium* X *cultorum*. Usually this impressive plant is resplendent in all shades of blue, but there are white, mauve, and pink varieties.

It is best to buy young plants in early summer, or you can sow seeds in April. Larkspur needs a sunny site and a soil really rich in nutrients if it is to develop properly. Fertilizer should only be added in the spring. In the summer, be courteous to the plant and give it a support to stop it toppling over under the weight of its flowers. Water copiously.

If larkspur is cut back right after flowering, it may repay you in the fall with extra flowers.

You can propagate by digging your larkspur up in spring or fall, carefully dividing it, and replanting the parts — it's very simple.

A warning from the plant doctor: greedy slugs and snails love larkspur as much as we do!

Lily

The ultimate classic!

What it is:
- a magnificent plant grown from a bulb
- grows 16 inches to 5 feet tall, depending on type and variety
- flowers from May through September, depending on type and variety
- flowers can be white, salmon pink, yellow, and orange
- hardy and robust (zones 3–8)

What it needs:
- sun to semishade
- well-drained lime soils
- protection from late frosts

Scientific name:
Lilium

There is something noble about the lily, with its elegant bell-shaped flowers. It radiates sophistication and an aura of the sublime, and yet it's quite happy in a pot on the balcony. Best of all, most lilies are fairly hardy.

There are many beautiful types and varieties. Our tip is the truly royal *Lilium regale*. You can make a real impression with this one. In July it produces scented white blooms with a delicate touch of pink. Or try the Madonna lily, *Lilium candidum*. It is snow-white, scented, and grows to a height of three feet. Or the fire lily, *Lilium bulbiferum,* with bright, glowing orange blooms, that grows up to 40 inches in height.

Plant the bulbs in the fall in the open air or in a deep pot or container (at a depth of six inches). Don't leave the bulbs lying around for too long after purchase. Lilies look their best when planted in groups, spaced at 12–20 inches, depending on type and variety. Standard potting mix is fine. The soil should be loose, because lilies don't like too much moisture. They need plenty of sun while growing, at least on the flowers and leaves, but direct, blazing midday sun is not right either. The ground should be nice and cool, moist and shady, so see about some under-planting, of Erigeron (page 136) perhaps? They do make quite a few demands on you, lilies.

Flowering time is from May through September, depending on type and variety. Support long stalks a little after flowering. Wait until they are brown and withered until you cut them off and you can look forward to next summer (the lily grows from a bulb so it is a perennial).

In cold growing zones, cover less hardy plants with a few twigs in winter. This will protect the emerging new leaves in spring against late night frosts.

A warning from the plant doctor: we are not the only ones with a weakness for lilies. Snails and slugs love the plant too, and will eat it down to the roots if they get the chance.

Stock

Charming, charming

What it is:
- annual, growing 16–32 inches high
- flowers from June through September…
- …in white, yellow, pink, red, and violet

What it needs:
- sunshine
- regular watering…
- …but don't let the roots get waterlogged

Scientific name:
Matthiola incana

This little guy is really delightful, with all those frilly flowers in white, yellow, pink, red, and violet. It has been flowering most attractively in gardens since our grand-mothers' time.

Sow it in February–March; it does best in sandy soil. Or buy stock seedlings from the garden center from April onward. Then put them into a pot or into the flower bed, planting them four inches apart.

Stock is usually planted as a border or bedding plant. Some species emit a wonderful fragrance at night.

Stock gets very upset if saturated. All in all, this plant prefers to be dry and warm. Then you can enjoy the flowers from June through September.

Malope

Delightful, relaxed, easy to plant

What it is:
- annual, up to 40 inches high
- flowers from July through October
- white, pink, or red blooms
- completely problem-free

What it needs:
- sunshine
- and that's all there is to it

Scientific name:
Malope trifida

Where's the catch? Something this beautiful can't be this easy and hardy. Oh yes it can! Just give your malope sunshine, and the rest will follow; namely, glorious, delicate flowers, round, silky, and colorful in white, pink, and red, blooming incessantly in superb abundance. Not everything has to have a catch.

Sow malope in April, either in the garden or in a window box, wherever you want them to flower. Then thin out the seedlings to 12–16 inches apart. Because they grow up to four feet tall, these plants are ideal gap-fillers in the garden and good for hiding the compost heap or a fence.

Malope will grow in any kind of soil, but prefers sandy loam. It really needs lots of sunshine which will encourage it to flower. All you need to do then is water copiously and feed every 6 weeks.

What to plant with it:
Mix malope in a window box with other low-growing flowers. Never plant this robust Mediterranean plant next to the true mallow (*Malva* spp.) because the latter are susceptible to mallow rust and there is a danger of infection.

Window sill Tip:
They stay fresh in a vase!

Bellflower

This could be my summer infatuation

What it is:
- fast-growing, bushy perennial, biennial, or annual
- flowers from June till August…
- …in white, pink, blue, or violet
- robust, but not hardy (zones 3–8)

What it needs:
- sun or semishade
- a little water

Scientific name:
Campanula spp.

This plant brings a real summer atmosphere with its delicate flowers ranging in color from white to pink, blue to violet. Bellflowers can soon develop into carpets of blooms. And they are very easy to care for.

In spring, buy plants or grow them from seed. When buying, look out for type and variety. You can get them hardy (*Campanula garganica*). The blue Dalmatian bellflower (*Campanula portenschlagiana*) is ideal for growing in pots, as it is only 6 to 10 inches tall. Whichever species you choose, you can put them outside from April onward (plant them 12 to 16 inches apart).

Bellflowers grow in any ordinary garden soil. They are happy if they get warmth and sunshine, need little water, and positively dislike being saturated. Adding fertilizer every four weeks is enough. Occasionally, you need to remove dead flowers. And that's all!

Propagate bellflowers from seed or by dividing the roots in spring (page 20–21). Easy!

73

There are specialist gardeners in every field, even in early-flowering plants. Snowdrops start things off in February, and then crocuses take over until the end of March. Daffodils, narcissi, and tulips carry on the good work right through into May.

Crocus

Really early, really colorful, really Basic

What it is:
• easy-to-care-for bulb
• early starter, flowering from the end of February...
• ...in lots of colors
• comes back year after year (zones 4–8)

What it needs:
• sunshine
• no waterlogging
• no late frosts

Scientific name:
Crocus imperati, Crocus vernus, Crocus tommasinianus

Crocuses grow vertically to about four inches in height. The flowers are white, yellow, pink, deep purple, lavender, or violet, and may be one color or striped. They bring a colorful glow to the end of winter and are easy to care for and hardy.

You can buy flowering crocuses in late February and plant them out, or you can take the trouble to plant bulbs in groups in September – October in containers or in the flower beds (4 inches apart, depth of planting 2 to 3 inches). Crocuses in window boxes like standard potting mix; those in flower beds prefer loamy, humus-rich soils.

Potted plants like to be watered from time to time; do not let them dry out. When the first new shoots appear, put them in the light and water moderately. Be careful, they do not like being saturated. They flower in February and March.

Snowdrop

Harbinger of spring

What it is:
• a bulb
• classic herald of warmer weather
• white flowers appear in February
• reliable, flowering year after year

What it needs:
• a light-to-semishady spot
• and that's about it
• in winter, garden plants need winter protection, potted plants a frost-free and light spot

Scientific name:
Galanthus nivalis (for the garden)
Galanthus elwesii (for growing in pots)

At last, the few bright days after the turn of the year. You can buy flowering snowdrops for your balcony or garden everywhere from February onward. Or you can grow them yourself in September. Plant bulbs in containers (1 to 2 inches apart, 4 inches deep). Then leave them over the winter. Outdoors, cover them with spruce branches. Indoors, leave them in a cool, dark place. It is important not to let the soil dry out completely, even in winter.

When the first shoots emerge in spring, move them to a bright spot and keep them moist. Feed only twice during the growing period, and snip off dead parts of plants.

Window sill Tip:
You can get ready-grown snowdrops (and other early flowers such as crocus, tulips, or daffodils) for indoors as early as January.

Tulip

Maximum color,
zero-stress care

What it is:
• bulb
• flowers from March through May
• 6–24 inches tall, depending on the variety
• member of a large plant genus

What it needs:
• sunshine
• moderate watering, no waterlogging
• feeding once before flowering
• no late frost or there'll be trouble!
(zones 5–7)

Scientific name:
Tulipa spp.

Tulips come in almost any color. And there are so many varieties that everyone, from conservative to rebellious, will find something to their taste, from the scented woodland tulips (*Tulipa sylvestris*) to the golden yellow classic 'Bellona'; from the lily-like flowers of 'Queen of Sheba' to dwarf tulips (*Tulipa humilis* 'Persian Pearl'). There are wild tulips, hybrids of *Tulipa kaufmanniana*, that flower as early as March. Tulips are a real gardening Basic.

Plant the tulip bulb in the fall (by October at the latest) in flower beds or window boxes (1–2 inches deep). Tulips like sunny locations, only moderate amounts of water (avoid saturation), and a good helping of fertilizer once before flowering.

After flowering, cut off the dead stalks, but otherwise leave the plants alone. This makes for just the right amount of gardening stress that Basic Gardeners love.

Narcissus

So beautiful and yet so
easy — ideal for Basic
Gardening

What it is:
• yet another early-flowering bulb
(zones 4–8)
• grows 8 inches to 2 feet high, depending on the variety
• flowers from February through May, depending on the variety...
• ...in shades of yellow, orange, and white, and even in two colors

What it needs:
• sunshine to semishade
• well-drained soil...
• ...and no waterlogging

Scientific name:
Narcissus spp.

In Greek mythology, Narcissus was a very handsome guy — and he knew it. When this arrogant creep dumped the nymph Echo, the goddess Aphrodite decided to pay him back and cursed him with a completely hopeless love affair. The poor fellow fell in love with his own reflection, which was bound to be a rather one-sided affair in the long run. Not until he was turned into a flower did his unhappy love come to an end. Sigmund Freud based a famous psychoanalytical theory on this story. "God, do I look good!" types have since been called "narcissists."

We all know some species of narcissus (and probably a few narcissists too). The tall yellow-flowered daffodil is one. So is the lenten lily. So is the poet's narcissus with its white, scented star-shaped flowers.

Plant bulbs in fall (the large, multiple ones to a depth of 6–8 inches, smaller ones shallower and 8 inches apart). Water during the growing phase and the flowering period. After flowering, simply leave them alone, and they will propagate enthusiastically. They won't need any further attention during the winter, either.

Window sill Tip:
You can often buy narcissus from January onward, frequently already in flower, for growing indoors.

These three plants, black-eyed Susan, clematis, and climbing hydrangea, all have attractive, strong personalities. After all, they are professional climbers. Some are ramblers, others prefer something to hold on to, but they will easily grow 40 to 80 inches every summer.

Black-eyed Susan

Look me in the eye!

What it is:
- climbing bedding plant
- grows up to 80 inches
- bright orange, yellow, and white flowers ...
- from June through October

What it needs:
- sunshine and warmth
- no rain or wind

Scientific name:
Thunbergia alata

There's something about this Susan. She's a big girl — up to seven feet tall — and remarkably good looking, with many brilliant white, yellow, or orange flowers. And she's got class, with that black eye in the middle of the flower.

This plant is a Basic because it grows so fast, flowers repeatedly from June through October, and looks good anywhere. It climbs when given something to support it. If not, it acts as a hanging plant, which is just as attractive.

Sow in early March (3–4 seeds per pot). The pots should be placed in a sunny and warm location; they like room temperature. The seeds will germinate in about three weeks. Pinch off the tips and they will grow more densely (page 26).

When they show a good strong growth, put baby Susans into a window box or plant them 16–20 inches apart in open air, but not until after the last frost. Water evenly, feed every two weeks, and keep away from wind and rain (under the eaves of a roof, for instance).

In the summer, black-eyed Susan can easily be propagated. Take cuttings and, in pleasant, warm summer weather, place them in moist sand under an upside-down glass tumbler. They soon take root (pages 20–21).

In colder zones you will only be able to keep the plants for one summer. However, you can let them winter indoors (transplant into small pots and place them in a well-lit room that is very slightly heated). In February, prune the plants thoroughly.

Clematis

So, so romantic!

What it is:
- perennial climbing plant (zones 4–9)
- 7–40 ft high depending on type and variety
- flowers from June through September
- produces large, multicolored flowers
- some varieties flower in a cascade

What it needs:
- sunshine to semishade
- warmth and sunshine at the top, where the flowers are
- cool and moist at ground level
- winter protection for potted plants in colder zones

Scientific name:
Clematis
Variety Tip: *Clematis montana rubens*, a lush climbing beauty with rosy pink blooms

The clematis is probably the prettiest vine (we're not just saying that; as a climber, it is a true vine) in our garden. This plant has very decorative, flat, large, gorgeous, white, pink, blue, or violet blooms up to six inches in diameter.

If you want to grow clematis, you have quite a choice. You can choose from spring-flowering varieties, such as the deep pink *Clematis montana* 'Superba', (20 –25 feet high) or

wait until high or late summer for *Clematis jackmanii* to produce deep purple flowers or for the dark blue flowers of 'Gipsy Queen', both of which grow to 10–13 feet. There are also varieties such as *Clematis paniculata*, with its white, scented flower clusters that appear from September through October (40 feet high). Some look like pink cascades and even climb over walls (*Clematis montana rubens,* for instance).

East- and west-facing locations are better than those facing north or south.

Whichever variety you choose, they all like well-drained soil, so don't let them get water-logged. If you plant clematis in the garden, dig a hole about 20 inches deep. First put in a layer of gravel (about a hand's breadth in depth). Plant the clematis deeply, but do not plant it upright, but at an angle, while you re-fill the hole with soil. Now trail the shoot some 12 inches across the soil away from the plant and cover it with a layer of soil, about four inches deep. Not until it has covered this distance can you allow it back into the fresh air. Why? Because clematis likes it that way, that's why. Afterwards, mulch, and don't forget to provide a climbing support (wire or trellis).

Clematis was originally a forest plant, of course. That is why it likes its roots to stay moist but it likes the magnificent flowers to be in warm sunshine. You can manage this

with a simple trick. Plant low-growing shrubs or ground-cover plants in front of your clematis. Important pruning information: do not prune spring-flowering plants in March, or you will cut off the flower buds. Summer-flowering plants, on the other hand, could do with a good prune in March.

What to plant with it:
Plant wild grapes with clematis — they make a fantastic couple.

Climbing hydrangea

Very easy

What it is:
• perennial woody climber (zone 4)
• shiny green oval leaves ...
• ... and large white flower clusters in June and July
• grows up to 35 feet in height

What it needs:
• semishade to sun
• well-drained soil

Scientific name:
Hydrangea petiolaris

The climbing hydrangea has a natural personality, just the thing for a loosely designed garden, close to nature. With its shiny green leaves and blossoms, it covers walls and fences. It is also ideal for dark city gardens with ugly walls. And it looks good as ground-cover.

And because this plant wants nothing else from us — no care, no pruning — we are awarding it the Basic Gardening merit prize for 100% easy care.

Buy it in spring, from the garden center or nursery, and plant it out. Climbing hydrangeas like well-drained soil and prefer some protection from scorching sun. They produce brilliant white blooms in June and July.

Take care to provide moisture at first. After a few years, the plant will be able to cope with the odd dry spell as well.

Pruning: none at all, just thin it out a little in spring.

One further point: because of their clinging roots, some landlords don't like them, as they could damage the facade of the building. Clear it with the landlord in advance.

At last, the plant doctor is happy. Hydrangea is highly resistant to snails and slugs.

The following fabulous four are the essence of blossom, scent, and summer. May we introduce the hydrangea, phlox, lilac, and plumbago.

Common hydrangea

Makes a few demands, but it's worth it

What it is:
- shrub growing up to 8 feet high, depending on variety
- lush flowers from May to July (zone 5)
- blooms like round balls, flat clusters, or narrow spikes, depending on the variety...
- ...in white, pink, red, blue, and violet

What it needs:
- semishade
- moist, well-drained soil
- plenty of watering ...
- ... with softened water
- rhododendron food every two weeks until August
- protection in colder zones during winter

Scientific name:
Hydrangea macrophylla

These hydrangeas originate from Asia, where for centuries they have been among the flowering elite. They are a delight, especially in country-style gardens and they're not so fussy about sunshine. Although introduced into Europe and America, they have been here for so long that they are quite evidently considered to be classic plants as far as we are concerned.

After all, the main thing is that they look stunning and thrive, with a little care, in semishaded locations. That's ideal for city gardens. The plant, by the way, could be described as the shorter sister of the less well-known climbing hydrangea (page 77).

Take care when buying hydrangeas, there are so many varieties. *Hydrangea paniculata* 'Grandiflora' has a second spell of flowering in late summer and grows up to 10 feet tall.

You will need rich, moist soil for hydrangeas. For potted plants, you can buy rhododendron compost anywhere, but in the garden, you will have to give your soil a boost with mulch or leaf compost.

Water frequently. Hydrangeas need rhododendron fertilizer feeding every two weeks until August. It flowers between June and September, depending on the variety and weather conditions.

Never prune in spring, because the flowers grow on the new shoots. In fall, just nip off the dead flowers.

The plant doctor has no reason for complaint: hydrangeas are robust and resistant to snails and slugs.

Phlox

The essence of summer!

What it is:
- hardy perennial, up to 5 feet tall (zone 4)
- white, pink, orange, red, violet, and two-colored flowers ...
- ... depending on variety, from June through September
- fragrant and a favorite with butterflies

What it needs:
- sunshine and plenty of water
- loamy, nutrient-rich soil

Scientific name:
Phlox paniculata

'Amethyst', 'Starfire', 'Vintage Wine' are the names of some varieties, a reminder of the brilliantly colored flowers produced throughout the summer. Other lovely varieties include 'Nora Leigh' (variegated foliage and white flowers) and 'Elizabeth Arden' (pink). 'Starfire' is brilliant red and grows up to 3 feet.

Plant in the spring or fall, 20–36 inches apart. In early summer, this plant needs plenty of water and fertilizing. Cut off dead flowers immediately. Once it has bloomed, pinch out the first main flower stem, and then the side-shoots will bring plenty of follow-on flowers. If the phlox is getting old, it would do it good to be divided (pages 20–21).

Lilac

The scent of summer

What it is:
• the classic flowering shrub (zone 3) ...
• ... with scented blossom (but only after a few years) growing in elegant spikes ...
• ... from May till June
• 40 inches to 20 feet tall
• undemanding

What it needs:
• sunshine or light shade
• well-drained soil

Scientific name:
Syringa hybrids

Lilac is most famous for its intoxicating scent and for its elegant, elongated flower spikes, on which the white, lilac, or violet blooms appear. There are the classic lilac varieties, and these are hybrids that grow up to 20 feet tall and flower as early as May. The flowers may be white, pink, purple, or the classic mauve. There are also attractive, less formal-looking varieties, such as *Syringa chinensis*, which has purple flowers and grows up to 10 feet tall. Unfortunately, the flowering season for lilacs is relatively short.

Snip off all dead flower heads immediately. When the bush is older, at least two years old, it will happily accept pruning. This makes it very suitable to use as a hedge.

Plumbago

Needs attention, but is rewarding

What it is:
• perennial shrub with blue flowers ...
• ... on very long shoots
• flowers throughout the summer from June through October
• not hardy (zone 9)
• also looks good in pots

What it needs:
• sunshine and warmth
• no wind
• plenty of water
• feeding once a week until August
• pruning radically before winter
• wintering indoors

Scientific name:
Plumbago auriculata

Admittedly, plumbago sounds a bit like plumbing, but in fact it's nothing so ordinary. Looking at its long, delicate, elegant shoots, you can end up feeling dreamy and romantic. It has a touch of "Rapunzel, Rapunzel, let down your hair" about it.

Plumbago thrives best in the garden, especially if it has plenty of room to spread out. However, as balcony gardeners are aware, it can also produce a respectable show of flowers when grown in a pot.

You can also get plumbago as a tall standard (looks superb!), but these varieties are not inexpensive. The tall stems definitely need something to support them, because they are fragile and can't bear much weight. The branches also break easily, which is why it hates the wind. Plumbago is a good plant for a hanging basket, where it can let its flowers droop down and enjoy the protection from the eaves of a roof.

Plumbago needs a sunny, warm spot, plenty of watering, and feeding once a week up until August. During the flowering period, dead flowers should be snipped off from time to time. After flowering, cut it back rigorously.

Plumbago prefers to spend the winter in a pleasantly temperate environment; ideally, in a slightly heated room. It doesn't care whether the room is light or dark. If dark, however, cut the plant right back to ground level before moving it, and keep it almost dry.

You need to take some care with this plant. But when conditions are right, it will reward you with a mass of blooms.

Fruit trees are a subject in their own right, from savvy shopping to proper planting, and most importantly, advice on care. For basic information on fruit trees, see page 69.

Apple tree

A Super-Basic!

What it is:
• miniature fruit tree that can also be grown in containers
• just right for city gardens and balconies ...
• ... because it only grows to 7 feet
• available in many varieties
• can produce up to 20 pounds of apples

What it needs:
• humus-rich, moist soil
• winter protection for trees in tubs (zones 3–9)

Scientific name:
Malus

An apple tree on my balcony? And even fruit? That would be nice, but how do I do it?

It's very easy. For instance, using a miniature apple tree. It grows to a maximum of seven feet in height. You'll have room for it in the smallest garden or yard or in a pot on the tiniest balcony.

Buy these trees only from a specialist supplier and take good advice, because apple trees only fruit in the company of other apple trees. When to buy them? Anytime — but most effectively in late summer and fall, when they are bearing fruit.

You can also buy apple tree duos; for instance, dwarf trees that bear the popular varieties ' Golden Delicious' and 'Cox's Orange Pippin' on the same tree.

Plant the apple trees in a sunny spot. The soil should not be wet and cold, but not too dry either. Provide a support for the first two years. Plant in the garden 20 inches apart.

In spring, add long lasting fertilizer (dosage according to instructions). Or from spring to the end of June, add organic liquid feed every 2–3 weeks.

From mid-May on, the apple tree will blossom. Fruits will be ripe, depending on variety, from September to October. Cover the pots in winter with leaves.

On the subject of apple trees, they make a really original gift, especially when there's a new arrival in the family — and they're particularly impressive with fruit on them.

Pear tree

So tempting!

What it is:
• a dream of a fruit tree
• as a single-stem, also suited to small city gardens and balconies
• only grows to 7–10 feet, including crown

What it needs:
• nutrient-rich, light soil
• rather too dry than too moist
• warmth and a protected location (zones 4–9)
• no waterlogging of the roots

Scientific name:
Pyrus communis
Tip: we recommend a dwarf fruit tree that bears two different fruit varieties (see below).

Another of the pleasures of late summer is sweet, yellow, lovely, juicy pears. What a good thing that you can get miniature pear trees for small spaces and balconies, either as single-stem trees or as the very special tree that bears two varieties of pear! At seven feet high, it is just the right size for balconies, perfectly container-compatible, and very easy to handle. And a duo certainly catches the eye! What will these plant breeders think of next? You can get duos in the varieties 'Doyenne de Comice' (yellow) and 'Conference' (greenish-yellow). These varieties keep well.

Excellent for making home-grown, home-baked fruit flans and for drying in slices.

Even miniature pear trees have roots that go deep. The container should be deep enough for them — at least 20 inches. Pear trees, whether a single variety or duo form, need a warm location, and trees in pots need protection from rain. Feed in spring and summer, every 2–3 weeks, using organic liquid fertilizer.

Pear blossom time is in May. Harvest time is early through mid-September.

In winter, cover the pots with leaves, since the duos are particularly sensitive to frost.

Cooking Tip:

What to do with an over-abundant crop? Store fresh fruit in the cellar if you have one. Or you can arrange apple rings and wedges of pear on a cookie sheet and dry them for 1-2 hours in a slightly open oven with the temperature at 125°F.

Sweet cherry

The taste of summer

What it is:
• miniature cherry only grows to 13 feet in height — properly pruned, to only 8 feet
• frost-resistant

What it needs:
• a support
• not much water ...
• ...except in dry summers
• another cherry tree for cross-pollination

Scientific name:
Prunus avium

Picking sweet, juicy red cherries from your own tree in summer and spitting the stones into your own garden — what a delight! Up until now, this was reserved only for people with really large gardens. If you have a small garden, or yard, you can now get a sweet cherry tree which stays nice and small, 'Lambert's Compact'.

'Lambert's Compact' is a bush-like tree and with clever pruning it only grows to 8 feet, but even without it is only 12 feet, comparatively small for a strongly growing cherry tree.

When buying, be sure to ask at your nursery which variety of fruit will provide you with sweet cherries. The cherry will only fruit if the right varieties are planted together. Those recommended for a good crop include 'Hedelfinger', 'Sam', 'Van', and the Morello cherry. But if you want only one tree in your garden instead of two, try this trick. In spring, simply put a vase of wild cherry blossom next to the tree on your balcony — that's often quite enough.

Sweet cherries are undemanding in terms of soil type. However, the soil should not be too wet, cold, or heavy. Plant the trees 10 feet apart and immediately tie the sapling to a solid supporting stake. The miniature sweet cherry will need this support all its life.

These trees don't need much water. They only need plenty of watering in dry summers, as the roots often don't reach very deep into the ground.

Cherries can often be picked as early as one year after planting, in June – July. This is great news for impatient gardeners and for those who like to eat well. In four years' time, a tree may produce around ten pounds of fruit, and as much as thirty pounds after ten years.

Wild flowers

The purity of nature

What it is:
• a meadow in your window box ...
• ... full of wild flowers ...
• ... and as attractive to people ...
• ... as it is to butterflies, bees, and others

What it needs:
• sunny, open location
• regular watering
• little care

Scientific name:
None, ask for wildflower meadow seeds

Weeds can look so beautiful. A butterfly meadow full of scarlet poppies, cornflowers, and hare's tail grass — pure joy! These plants grow everywhere; beside railroads, on construction sites, at the roadside. And, of course, where we live. It's a little miniature oasis for us and for the butterflies, who can't survive on lawns that have been weeded and fertilized to within an inch of their lives. This is how you do it.

Buy the seed mixture in March. Ecologically minded gardeners should ensure that it not only includes colorful flowers, but also plants on which caterpillars feed (essential if you want caterpillars to turn into butterflies); for example, a butterfly-friendly mixture.

We also recommend a mixture for dry locations, which includes ox-eye daisies, clover, and bird's-foot trefoil. But for damp locations, the mixture should include violets, sorrel, and sweet cicely.

You will need a handful of seed mixture for a window box about two feet long. By the way, it is very easy to create a wildflower meadow in a window box — but in the garden, it requires quite a lot of care and attention. Starting with the soil, which should not be too rich because a wildflower meadow mix is a "lean" mixture. The plants are dying out for the very reason that everyone is fertilizing the fields as if there were no tomorrow. If you have a full-time job, or any other large commitment, we recommend that you don't put a wildflower meadow in your garden.

Gently press down the earth in your window box and sprinkle it with the seeds, but not too thickly. Crumble some soil over them and press down lightly with a board. Water well initially. And go gently, gently! Then stand the box in the shade and keep it moist. As soon as the first shoots appear, move it into the light. In June, when the whole splendor of flowers is revealed, your wild specimens could even manage the full sun.

Afterward, keep watering well and feeding from time to time. If the grass in the box becomes too thick, trim the "meadow" to about four inches with garden shears.

Oriental poppy

Straight out of a Monet painting

What it is:
• perennial, grows up to 32 inches
• white, salmon pink, and red flowers
• flowers May through June
• tough and hardy (zone 3)

What it needs:
• lots of sunshine and lots of space
• good, nutrient-rich earth

Scientific name:
Papaver orientale

The scarlet wild poppy is an annual that is often included in wildflower mixtures, but some poppies are perennial. These are known as oriental poppies and are available in many varieties. Oriental poppies make some demands on their environment, which must be sunny, but not wet. They want only the finest, nutrient-rich soil and need frequent feeding, as well as space in which to develop.

It is best to buy young plants in spring or fall and plant them in groups. After flowering (May–June), cut the flower stalks back to ground level. New leaves will grow right into the fall.

Cornflower

Pure nostalgia

What it is:
• annual garden plant, and not only with blue flowers
• related to the wild cornflower
• flowers from July through September
• 16–40 inches tall, depending on variety

What it needs:
• sunshine
• poor soil

Scientific name:
Centaurea

Cornflowers are usually bright blue, but you can also get them in white, pink, and purple. Some of the varieties are 'Jolly Joker' (lilac or pink), 'Snowman' (pure white), 'Blauer Junge' (blue), and 'Pinkie' (pink, what else could it be?).

Sow them outdoors in March in the garden or in planters, and later thin out the seedlings and space them at 10 inches apart. They flower from July through September, but once summer fades, so does the magic of the cornflower.

What to plant with it:
Cornflowers prefer poor soils and therefore go well with hare's tail grass, corn marigolds, and chamomile.

Hare's tail grass

Elegant

What it is:
• very decorative annual...
• ... with soft flowers and leaves

What it needs:
• sunshine
• poor soil
• moderate watering
• no fertilizing and no further care

Scientific name:
Lagurus ovatus

Grasses are natural beauties that bring a touch of nature into our city gardens. They are, after all, among the oldest plant life on our planet and have hardly changed through breeding, which shows in their strength and timelessly beautiful appearance. Grasses look superb among wild shrubs and are undemanding. It is important to provide grasses with a suitable location in the garden, because they have different requirements. Some love cool, shady forests, others prefer hot, dry plains, yet others love swamps and bayous.

The elegant hare's tail grass loves dry sunny places and is an ideal partner for wildflowers, such as cornflowers and poppies. In the summer, it has velvety soft flowers (hence its name) and grows into little islands of grass about 16 inches across.

To grow hare's tail grass, put seeds into several small pots (handy if you want to combine it later with other plants in a window box) in April or sow directly in the window box or flower bed. Or buy young plants (plant them 8 inches apart). This grass needs a lot of sun and, like all wildflowers, prefers poor garden soil. Do not put potting mixture into the window box or hole without first mixing it with one-third sand.

Hare's tail grass doesn't need a lot of watering, but it shouldn't be allowed to dry out either. Feeding — no thanks, not necessary. Flowering is from June through August.

The plant doctor is happy. This grass has no pests and no diseases.

Styling Tip:
Do it all in grass. Plant hare's tail grass with grains or cat's tail grass in a container or pot — very stylish. Or try it with the colorful wild meadow mixture of cornflowers, poppies, and chamomile.

83

Delight your senses with sweet peas, scented geraniums, and wallflowers.

Sweet pea

Attractive and full of character

What it is:
• annual summer-flowering plant
• a talented climber
• grows up to 20 inches in its dwarf form
• grows up to 7 feet in its largest variety
• scented flowers in (nearly) all the colors of the rainbow

What it needs:
• sun but not burning, midday heat
• no wind
• climbing support

Scientific name:
Lathyrus odoratus

Sweet peas flower from June to September in almost all the colors of the rainbow, from pink and white to red, violet, and blue. They only last a single summer, but over those few months they grow up to 7 feet tall. In order to be able to do this, however, they need a fence, strings, or wires to hang on to.

You can buy them in the spring as young plants, or you can grow them from seed. Sow in February–March in individual pots or directly outdoors into a window box in April, planting them 4 inches apart. They don't like being transplanted, so plant them exactly where you want them.

Keep them good and moist, and feed weekly. Cut off dead flowers and new buds will emerge for more flowering.

The plant doctor warns that the seeds of sweet peas are poisonous. Sweet pea, itself, is threatened by spider mites, mildew, and gray mold.

Styling Tip:

Fancy a curtain of fragrance? It's quite simple; just sow a sweet pea mixture and have the plants climb up some stretched strings. It looks magical and smells like the summer of the century.

Scented geranium

An oasis for the nose!

What it is:
• spreading perennial ...
• ... with scented leaves in many fragrances
• easy to care for and looks good in a tub or container

What it needs:
• sun to semishade
• moderate watering
• to be indoors in winter (zone 10)

Scientific name:
Pelargonium Fragrans Group
There are many varieties, all with different fragrances.

This plant's country sisters, ordinary geraniums, have a rather bucolic air. If you like your flowers more cosmopolitan and sophisticated, try scented geranium. They have a much more elegant growth with more delicate flowers and, all in all, are really special. If you touch them gently, they smell quite wonderful. Some smell of pineapple, others of lemon, apple, or rose with a hint of cinnamon. They're a dream!

You can propagate these scented wonders in the summer using cuttings (pages 20–21).

Scented geraniums, whether bought as growing plants or home-grown, can be transplanted into a flower bed. Plant them 16 inches apart. In the open air, they need loam and sandy soils; in a pot they need standard potting mixture. After planting, water a lot but avoid saturation. Feed twice a week through the end of August.

Prepare them for the winter at the end of October by removing all dead flowers and pruning the whole plant down to half its size. It should not be too wet when moved into winter quarters (these should be cool and light; water it every now and then). Prune again in February. If you have a light, cool room available (perhaps an unheated guest room), keep your scented geranium there until mid-May, as the first stage of preparation for warmer times. After this, move it back to its sunny location.

Plant doctor's warning: watch out for aphids and whitefly.

Tip:
The lemon-scented variety is also suited to being grown as a bonsai (page 95).

Wallflower

So very green and flowers early

What it is:
• perennial but grown as biennial up to 12 inches tall ...
• ... with lush yellow and orange to light brown flowers
• early-flowering: April to June
• only worth keeping for one summer

What it needs:
• sunshine
• roots not waterlogged
• regular watering from March through May and feeding every two weeks
• winter protection for young plants (zone 6)

Scientific name:
Erysimum cheiri

Flowers in warm intense colors and has an intoxicating, sweet scent. Wallflowers are perhaps the prettiest way in the world of moving from spring to summer. Beds of scented wallflowers are especially effective. They also make a good edging for flower beds or paths and are a cheerful gap-filler among rigidly regimented tulips.

The gloriously brilliant wallflower is one of those summer flowers that does not bloom until its second year, so it is halfway between the short-lived summer flowers that last only one season and the perennials, which can live to a ripe old age.

You can buy them as early as March and plant them 8 inches apart. It is important to have well-drained soil, rich in nutrients. Wallflower roots hate being waterlogged. Water regularly while growing and feed lightly every two weeks.

If you want to raise wallflowers from seed, sow the seeds in warm soil between May and July. Since wallflowers only last for two years and only bloom in the second year, you will have to keep them safe in a harsh winter. Cover them with pine branches or twigs and do not allow them to dry out in the cold months. Only water on frost-free days.

The seeds are poisonous, so keep them away from children and pets.

Plant doctor's warning: watch out for mildew and gray mold.

Window sill Tip:
Wallflowers look great in a vase.

Miniature rose

Life is a bed of roses

What it is:
• just right for containers
• grows about 10–20 inches
• flowers from early summer through fall, depending on the variety ...
• ... in every color except blue

What it needs:
• plenty of sun
• an airy location; it doesn't mind wind ...
• ... but hates too much heat ...
• ... and absolutely no waterlogging
• to be fed once a week until July
• nutrient-rich soil (rose mixture)
• in colder zones, either protect it well outdoors or move into the house in winter

Scientific name:
Rosa

Recommended varieties: 'Baby Darling' (orange-pink, double blooms), 'Cinderella' (double pink and thornless), 'Lemon Delight' (semidouble, clear yellow)

It's true that roses are "born to be wild" and so prefer to be in the garden. It's obvious that, being deep-rooted, they're happiest when they have lots of soil beneath them. Fortunately, there are other varieties, so

that we "balconauts," who only have pots to offer, can also enjoy roses to the fullest. Which in turn makes us really happy. So, go to the garden center, ask for the sweet, little miniature roses for balconies and patios, buy them, buy some supplies, and take them home.

Pots for roses should be deep (about 16 to 20 inches). Roses need good, rich, but light soil, containing plenty of humus, loam, and sand. A special rose-growing mixture is available from nurseries and garden centers. They also need an airy, sunny spot or they will become diseased.

You can buy and plant roses all year round (space miniatures at least 12 inches apart), but spring and fall are best for planting. Pile a little soil around the young plants (take care that the thick grafting point on the rootstock is covered with soil) and water freely at first.

Watering should be regular, but moderate. Feed once a week from March through July. It is important not to let roses get waterlogged. Dead-head them regularly.

In colder zones in winter, roses in the garden need protection, so cover them with pine branches. Container roses also need protection. It is best to place individual pots in a large container and surround them with gravel, then wrap them up well in pine branches, or bring them into the house and

let them spend the winter in a cool, dark, airy place.

In spring, remove the upper layers of soil from the pot and replace with fresh earth. Once the first shoots appear, trim them back (page 68) and place the pot outdoors, but not right in the full sun, because roses like to take their time getting used to the outdoor life again.

You can propagate miniature roses by cuttings (page 20–21) from mid-August through mid-September.

The plant doctor's advice on roses can be found on page 68.

Dog rose

Magnificent hedging material

What it is:
• lush climbing rose that forms luxuriant hedges
• shoots grow up to 15 feet
• many varieties available
• flowers in June
• not sensitive to frost (zone 3)

What it needs:
• sunshine and nothing more

Scientific name:
Rosa canina

You couldn't have a more beautiful hedge. The dog rose, with its delicate flowers (yellow ring around the center, white in the center, and blushing pink toward the outer edge) always looks attractive and summery on fences, in garden corners, and as a living screen to hide whatever needs to be hidden. Its shoots can grow up to 15 feet tall and, after a while, will form graceful arches.

Plant in spring and leave it to get on with it. To make a hedge, leave a 5-foot gap between several plants. Every now and then you can (indeed you must) cut it back so that it doesn't smother everything.

In the fall, the elongated, dark red hips appear. You can make them into a very vitamin-rich jam, jelly or preserve, but cut them open and remove the seeds and hairs around them, which are an irritant.

Frost protection in winter? Not required!

The plant doctor's advice about roses can be found on page 68.

Climbing rose

A proud beauty that wants to be admired — and quite right, too

What it is:
• a flowering dream with large velvety blooms all through the summer in many colors
• grows up to 15 feet
• suited to living in a container
• hardy and tough

What it needs:
• sunshine
• a climbing support
• a deep pot
• and that's all

Scientific name:
Rosa

Recommended varieties: 'New Dawn' (pink, scented, luxuriant flowers), 'Gold Star' (golden yellow, luxuriant flowers)

Especially recommended: 'Super Dorothy', a climbing rose grafted onto tall standard stems; another pretty rose available as a tall standard is 'The Fairy' (photo above left). Also highly recommended: 'Mme. Alfred Carrière', cream-colored, fairly resistant to exhaust fumes, so ideal for city gardens.

Our favorite climber is 'Sympathie', which outdoes them all (see photo, above right). Its scarlet blooms can be admired throughout the summer, but it is hardy and barely susceptible to disease at all. The name 'Sympathie' doesn't quite hit the nail on the head for this variety (well, that isn't quite the right word either for its human equivalents such as Brad Pitt or Cindy Crawford).

Plant climbing roses in the spring. If they are to be grown in containers, they really need to be big and very deep (about 20 inches in diameter and just as deep). Climbers need some support, in the form of a trellis or wires.

Problems with disease? Advice from the plant doctor is on page 68.

Styling Tip:
Climbing roses are ideal for casting in romantic roles, such as rambling over arches or pergolas.

Where there's light there's shade; unfortunately, the reverse of this statement isn't true. Where there's shade, it doesn't mean there has to be light. At least not in our case. We have no light, but plenty of high-rise shade from an apartment block across the road that denies us the sun. Does that mean that we have to do without plants? No, it doesn't! Fortunately, there are plants that exist for every shady balcony.

Astilbe

As exotic as its name

What it is:
- hardy perennial (zones 3–5)
- grows from 20 inches to 4 feet tall
- flowers from July through September ...
- ... in white, pink, and dark red

What it needs:
- definitely no warmth or sun ...
- ... but semishade to shade

Scientific name:
Astilbe x arendsii

The individual flowers are tiny, but massed together they are impressive and decorative on their tall, feathery, bushy spikes. Depending on the variety, they can be white, pink, or deep red.

Astilbes grow up to 4 feet tall. There are some small, easy-to-handle, dwarf astilbes for window boxes. The simplest thing is to buy plants and plant them in a planter or window box from April onward, 8 inches apart or 20 inches apart in the garden. It goes without saying that the location should be moist, best of all loamy, but not at all hot or dry. That's no problem in the cool growing zones. Add long lasting fertilizer once a year, best of all in the spring.

In colder zones, astilbe will overwinter in the garden with a light layer of leaves as frost protection. Potted plants also usually survive the winter outdoors.

You can propagate astilbe by dividing the roots (pages 20–21)

What to plant with it:
A crazy combination: astilbes with ferns, grasses, and campanula.

Monkey flower

Just right for my north-facing balcony

What it is:
- annual summer flower
- grows 6–12 inches tall
- from June through September ...
- ... produces flowers in many different colors

What it needs:
- light to semishade ...
- airy and cool location
- moderate watering
- feeding once a week

Scientific name:
Mimulus hybrids

We've been waiting a long time for someone to share the dark side of our lives, and even enjoy it. So let's get going and buy some monkey flowers.

Monkey flowers bloom in yellow, cream, orange, red, and brown. They come dangerously striped like tigers or delicately spotted like a hen's egg. The flowers are shaped like small or large trumpets. The monkey flower has something of a miniature version of the orchid about it, sort of florid and

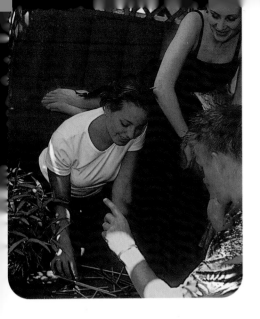

exotic, as if it just emerged from the jungle, yet it remains dainty and neat. And all this without a place in the sun, we can be thankful for that.

Impatient gardeners can start raising their monkey flowers as early as February, or you can wait until May and then sow them directly into a window box, 10 inches apart, in standard potting mixture. However, the quick way to your own monkey flower is as usual via the garden center. Simply buy ready-grown plants from April through July. Often they will already have their first flowers.

If you cut the tips off the young plants, they will grow back twice as thickly.

Afterward, water moderately. Monkey flowers like to be pleasantly moist all the time — and have a feed every week. Of course, they need to get their impressive looks from somewhere. After the first flowering, cut them back, then with any luck they will flower again for you.

Nightshade

Grows really big — and really impressive

What it is:
- luxuriant, flowering, fast-growing perennial (zone 9)
- ideal for balconies
- can grow up to 7 feet tall in containers
- purple flowers from May to October
- not hardy

What it needs:
- semishade
- plenty of water in summer
- feeding once a week until August
- to be taken indoors in winter

Scientific name:
Solanum rantonnetii
Synonym: "blue potato tree"

No-one likes to be alone at night. So get some nightshade. It will flower for you all throughout the summer, producing plenty of blue flowers, each with a little golden yellow eye in the center. It grows up to 7 feet, even in a container. The best thing about it is that it doesn't mind semishade. And if you leave it to its own devices, it will even start to climb. Something so splendid and in almost every respect so practical deserves to share our home with us.

Buy it in the spring. Put it in a sunny to semishady location, keep it nice and moist, and feed it once a week during the growing season.

In winter, put nightshade in the living root in a cool spot (a bright spot is better, but it will accept a dark one) and water it only occasionally.

Before moving it, give it a good prune (cut back down to 20 inches above the top of the pot). Repot in early March and move, if possible, to a lighter and warmer location, to let it prepare itself for summer.

More varieties:
Solanum jasminoides: Grows at turbo speed and, if it gets a constant supply of light, will produce shoots 35 feet long and clusters of flowers from spring to fall. Very robust.
Solanum muricatum: Good for hanging baskets, with its 40-inch long shoots and apple-sized, golden yellow fruits in August.

Special Styling

More is more

Be more daring and plant *en masse*! Mass is missing sometimes when you are in the garden center modestly packing one or two tiny plants into your shopping cart. Instead of a single lavender bush, try a field of lavender. Buy 20 plants and turn your window boxes into a genuine Provençal lavender field.

Anything goes

You can come out with kitsch — what a relief! — on your balcony, easily and successfully. The best way is to use Greek statues. Whether you pick Apollo (nude and life-size) or Aphrodite (plastic — supposed to look like marble and looks just like plastic) or Neptune (spewing water), even the smallest garden has space for a touch of the Acropolis.

Aluminum pails

If you aren't the romantic type, use aluminum pails from department stores as planters (by themselves or to hide the pots). You can get large ones and small ones, you can stand them or hang them up. They are winter-proof and have a touch of cool. On a covered balcony or patio, plants thrive in aluminum, as long as it has a drainage hole.

Hitchcock revival

Plastic crows, nice and big and scary and black, look frighteningly genuine and will keep unwanted birds away. They can be bought in garden centers and nurseries. Even in a window box, they can provoke a real Hitchcock-style shudder. Tippi Hedren would surely have loved them. We love them too.

More moss!

Admittedly, original Japanese moss garden landscapes are not easy to create. In this ancient garden tradition, moss is used as the design medium and covers stones, walls, and tree trunks. The skill is that the more artificial they are, the more natural the moss gardens look. The effect is a breath of deep peace.

Moss garden

Some tips for moss designs. First put a layer of sand, then bark mulch, and then finally a layer of loamy soil into a pot or in the garden, and plant the moss (*Polytrichum juniperninum*) on top. Essentials: shade, lots of water, no feeding (it will make green moss turn red and wilt). Mossy stones are symbols of long life.

Mini-Zen

No flowers, no trees, yet they are beautiful — Zen gardens. You, too, can make your own miniature Zen garden. Dig up a circle or rectangle and fill it with gravel. Smooth the gravel. Place a large and beautiful rock in the center and rake a pattern into the gravel around it. Use the rock as a meditation aid on the meaning of life.

Bamboo

The thick poles are particularly suitable for trellises (in Tokyo and Hong Kong they even make high-rise scaffolding out of them). Tie the poles together with weather-proof rope and reef knots, like this: put the right end over the left, knot; put the left end over the right, knot (well, okay, maybe you do need some practice, but after that ...).

Absence

Empty containers, whether terracotta amphorae, stone tubs, metal buckets, old tin tubs, or rustic barrels, all with nothing in them at all. According to the principles of Feng Shui, they are almost essential for any balcony or garden. Only if they are empty, completely empty, does the Universe have the chance to fill them with the owner's personal desires ...

Artful art

For real fakery, use Astroturf. No more trimming the lawn edges with nail scissors (no joke — we've seen it done). You can buy Astroturf by the yard in garden centers or even in carpet stores. It doesn't create dirt, doesn't need watering, hates lawn mowers, and has all the attraction and inimitable flair of genuine plastic.

Asia

All the mystery and wisdom of the East right in your flowerpots

Beautiful things come from Asia. Tatami mats, kimonos, rice paper lanterns. They are somehow simple, elegant, and esthetically pleasing. It's exactly the same with plants. Bamboo looks good. Period.

What's more, thousands of years of garden know-how come to us from Asia. Chinese farmers have been tending their land for thousands of years and many of them still produce crops today without artificial fertilizer, simply by closely observing nature. In ancient Japan, it was believed (and many Japanese still believe) that Nature is everywhere inhabited by the gods and trees are sacred. They believe that the whole world is a garden. It is for this reason that gardening is a highly regarded art form in Japan even today.

To enjoy an Asian balcony, complete with bamboo and azaleas, however, we need to appreciate Feng Shui, revisit Bali after a ten-year absence, or console ourselves with a Tai-Chi lesson at home (of course, we only need do these things if we feel so inclined).

But simply to have the desire to do these things is, in fact, quite sufficient.

Feng Shui Psychology Test

Too woody? Not fiery enough? Show me which plants you like and I'll tell you about yourself.

Feng Shui claims to be the ancient Far Eastern teaching of wisdom that concerns itself with achieving a state of harmony and balance (you should really tell the boss about it!). According to Feng Shui, all plants are assigned to the five elements: wood, fire, earth, water, and metal. And what is more, they have certain qualities that say something about us. So plants can be used as therapy and the balcony as the psychiatrist's couch, so to speak.

To take the test, find your favorite plants. The positive or negative qualities of the energy fields surrounding them will tell you what's the matter with you. Apart from Feng Shui, it can be left to the sound self-knowledge of Basic gardeners which of these attributes is likely to apply to them.

Wild Grape
A woody plant. Represents the spring, development, and change. People with a balance of wood energy are calm, sensitive, and just. And those whose energy is out of balance are angry, tense, and hypersensitive.

Clematis
An earth plant. Earth represents late summer, humidity, and abundance. People with positive earth vibrations are peace-loving, loyal, and reliable. Those with negative qualities are narrow-minded, unforgiving, and lacking in concentration.

Sunflower
A fire plant. Symbol of summer, growth, and speed. On the positive side: amusing, open, forward-looking, and self-assured. And the dark side, hyperactive, excitable, on edge, and a workaholic.

Foxtail Grass
A metal plant. Fall, dryness, and anything thick and tough pertain to the element metal. People with metal energy in harmony are honest, determined, intuitive, and fair. A lack of harmony makes a person severe, authoritarian, and uncompromising.

Lavender
A water plant. Qualities associated with the water element are winter, night, and cold. Water energy in the green area makes people calm, thoughtful, determined, and fearless. And in contrast: depressive, withdrawn, and anxious.

Styling Tip
Oriental fragrance

The Asian atmosphere spreads far and wide with garden joss-sticks. Everything you need for an outdoor orgy of fragrance from jasmine to lavender is available from Asian stores, decorator stores, and gift stores. Modern joss-sticks are bigger and thicker and burn for longer than the hippy, psychedelic kinds that were around in your mother's youth.

Another tip, seen in Chinese and Japanese stores: curtains for the balcony door, the Asian alternative to jangling plastic beads. They are made of plain linen fabric painted with a large black Chinese or Japanese character. Very unique, with an air of mystery.

Bonsai Basics

Ready for an ancient piece of Buddhist wisdom? "A prerequisite for the creation of a beautiful garden is a beautiful soul."

Only you and Judge Di

Reading tip for Asia fans: *The Cases of Judge Di* by Robert van Gulik. A district judge in Ancient China pursued criminals without benefit of karate acrobatics but with Taoist cunning. Gulik lived in China as a diplomat and scientist and wove many cultural and historical facts into his series. Very exciting and not too heavy-going, it is the ideal detective novel for a vacation on your Asian-style balcony.

Learning to meditate

The garden is the ideal place for meditation. At least this is the experience of Buddhists in their Zen monasteries who have meditated among trees and plants for hundreds of years. This is how to find happiness and contentment in the Here and Now and — perhaps if you meditate for long enough — Enlightenment. It also offers freedom from *dukkha* — in Buddhism that is everything that is unpleasant and painful, from a broken heart to tummy ache, and grief.

This is the best method to follow: In Zen monasteries, while meditating, prospective Buddhists
• rake leaves and pathways. It is easy to concentrate and do something useful.
• wander slowly through the garden
• pick a flower as an object on which to meditate. Observe its beauty, concentrate fully on this flower, and try to free the mind and spirit of everything extraneous.

What is bonsai?

Most garden centers and home-building stores carry bonsai trees. In its Japanese homeland, the raising and care of this miniature tree is, in fact, a demanding and meditative practice. The human being is at one with Nature and through deliberate trimming of the trunk, branches, twigs, and roots succeeds in creating a tiny tree less than three feet tall. As soon as the first shoot of the sapling appears, it is pruned, and it is then dependent on the skill of the tree designer. The branches are bent and twisted or screwed up tightly into unnatural positions. In creating bonsai art, the aim is to achieve the greatest clarity of form by the smallest means, with very few leaves and very few branches but all in a tightly ordered composition. Is it not much better to allow the tree to grow freely, rather than to subject it to so much manipulation? That is one point of view; it is up to you to decide.

How can you make a bonsai?

Bonsai are not house plants. If they are to be successful they must be outside.

Bonsai can of course be bought as small trees. As an art form and as an exercise in patience they are far from Basic, but growing them yourself is more interesting. Also popular with bonsai enthusiasts: plants that grow wild in woods and fields can be dug up provided you check first to ensure it is permitted.

What makes a good bonsai?

The following are suitable and grow as quickly as a bonsai can. (They need two or three years before they begin to take shape.) Birch (*Betula*), firethorn (*Pyracantha cocchinea*), honeysuckle (*Lonicera pileata*), willow (*Salix purpurea 'Nana'*), winter jasmine (*Jasminum nudiflorum*), and cotoneaster (*Cotoneaster microphyllus*).

Very important for bonsai beginners: cut off the most prolifically growing shoots throughout the summer, until about mid-August. Anyone who wants to master the art of bonsai should acquire the appropriate literature on the subject as a matter of priority. (Plenty is available at beginner level.)

And finally, an old Japanese bonsai saying: love simplicity and be satisfied with little.

Bamboo

To create the biggest impression

What it is:
• clumping bamboo with long, delicate, bright green leaves
• can grow to seven feet tall
• hardy and long-lived (zone 5)

What it needs:
• sunshine
• a sheltered spot
• watering sufficiently and regularly, enjoys a soak around the base
• in pots, feed once in the summer
• in the garden feeding is not necessary

Scientific name:
Thamnocalamus spathaceus

The most laid back of all the bamboo grasses. In contrast to the frost-sensitive weaklings of the family, it is hardy. It is very long-lived and is evergreen. It also grows very tall. What more could anyone want?

Bamboo can be bought as a small, medium, or large plant and replanted in the largest possible container or in the garden. Its favorite spot is sunny, sheltered from the wind, but damp rather than dry. Above all, care must be taken to ensure that the plant always gets enough to drink. So water it regularly and stand it in a deep tray; it is very partial to a footbath. As a pot plant, bamboo only needs feeding once during the summer. In the garden, feeding takes care of itself, as it fertilizes itself by means of its own rotted down leaves.

And once again, this bamboo variety, if lightly protected with straw and twigs, will survive winter in colder zones without any problems.

The plant doctor says: pests that attack bamboo are almost unheard of.

Stocks can be increased by division (pages 20–21).

Japanese sedge

Shade-loving

What it is:
- botanically a perennial, visually a grass
- undemanding and long lasting
- not a hardy perennial (zone 8)
- evergreen with curved yellow stripes on the leaves

What it needs:
- semishade to full shade
- scant watering
- do not soak the base
- 1–2 feeds per season
- winter protection with straw and twigs

Scientific name:
Carex morrowii

Green in summer and in winter. Seasons seem to pass by without leaving a trace. Its only vanity is a yellow stripe that adorns the center of the curved leaf and curves down to its tip. That is why the Japanese sedge wins a Basic Gardening award in the category of long lasting and undemanding.

The Japanese sedge is best purchased as a young plant and planted in pots, containers, or the garden. Its requirements are really modest. It flourishes in the shade, only needs

a small amount of water, and 1–2 feeds is fine over the summer. But don't keep it too damp and never drown it!

Window sill Tip:
The Japanese sedge is also suitable for indoors. It prefers a cool, shady location. Do not overwater it, keep it fairly dry.

Foxtail grass

Another exotic newcomer

What it is:
- remains green in mild zones. Delicate curved leaves
- long stems with reddish-brown flower-heads that look like ears of wheat
- hardy perennial (zone 5)

What it needs:
- a place in the sun
- damp soil and plenty of water

- feeding every two weeks from May through August
- winter protection with spruce branches in cold zones

Scientific name:
Pennisetum alopecuroides

An exotic grass with narrow, curving leaves and long flower stems which bear bushy, reddish-brown flower heads 8 inches long that look like ears of wheat. In Europe it is called lamp-cleaner grass because oil lamps were once cleaned with a brush this shape. This plant is prized for its esthetic qualities and oriental elegance.

It is best to buy small plants and plant them in pots, containers, or in the garden. The soil should be damp; sandy soils are unsuitable. Foxtail grass favors a sunny location, and as it hails from the tropics, it needs plenty to drink. So water regularly (above all, ensure that pot plants do not dry out). Feed it every two weeks from May through August.

This Asian grass will survive winter in colder zones if the roots are covered with straw and twigs.

The plant doctor is happy: foxtail grass is not subject to pests or diseases!

Stocks can be increased by division (pages 20-21).

Japanese flowering cherry

Lovely to look at

What it is:
• a very attractive tree...
• ..with delicate pink blossoms, starting late April through early May
• well-suited to small gardens — only grows 4 to 7 feet tall

What it needs:
• sunshine
• fertilizer once a season, in the spring before the blossoms appear

Scientific name:
Prunus serrulata
Recommended variety: 'Shidare-Sakura'

This is the best excuse for the first garden party of the year, at least in Japan, where they celebrate the Cherry Blossom Festival in all its ceremonial. Simply because it is such a beautiful sight. The 'Shidare-Sakura' is a particularly attractive ornamental variety whose delicate pink blossoms appear in late April through early May. It only grows four to seven feet at the most, so it is eminently suitable for a pot or small garden.

Plant in the garden either in March or in late fall (October). Make absolutely sure that you dig a hole that is large enough and around 16 inches deep. A sunny spot with soil that is not too damp is the perfect location. Give it a good feed after planting.

Japanese flowering cherry can easily withstand harsh winters. And with a life span of 20–30 years (after which it is often affected by disease) this ornamental cherry will provide a feast for the eyes for a long time.

Japanese azalea

Know exactly what they want

What it is:
• hardy shrub with magnificent flowers
• fully grown at four feet tall

What it needs:
• shade
• special rhododendron plant food (two feeds over the summer)
• acidic soil

Scientific name:
Rhododendron 'Hinodegiri'

This plant has wonderful flowers and is hardy enough to survive the winter. This small, tree like shrub with shiny green, leathery leaves is a springtime attraction, producing masses of flowers in white, pink, or red as early as April or May.

Buy Japanese azaleas ('Hinodegiri' has beautiful red flowers) and plant in a large pot or in the garden by late March or early April. If planting in a border or flower bed, dig a large hole, and put in the plant. Apart from that, the azalea needs as much shade as possible as it does not like full sun (causes spider mites and leaf curl). Water abundantly and regularly, and feed twice during the summer with rhododendron food.

The Japanese azalea will survive winter in colder zones if the tub is packed with straw and twigs.

Propagation? Not for novices!

What to plant with it:
Japanese azalea will not tolerate being planted next to spruce.

Hibiscus

Magic flower whose blooms only last for one day

What it is:
• grows to seven feet tall ...
• ... with dark green leaves and large funnel-shaped flowers
• flowers from June through September, but each bloom only lasts for one day

What it needs:
• a sunny, sheltered spot
• regular watering
• weekly feeding until August
• bringing indoors in winter (zone 5)

Scientific name:
Hibiscus syriacus

Each hibiscus bloom only lasts for one day. But don't worry, there are always new ones coming along. With its beautiful dark green, slightly serrated leaves and large funnel-shaped flowers, the hibiscus is the highlight of any tropical balcony. And from June through September the flowers produce lovely contrasting colors against the green (white through pink to blue and red, depending on the variety).

Buy hibiscus as small plants and plant in large pots (the shrub can grow to around

seven feet tall). From the end of May, place outside in the open air. Be sure to choose a sunny location sheltered from the wind and rain. Water it regularly and under no circumstances allow it to dry out. Feed it once a week until mid-August. It doesn't like soil that is too dry or cold or being moved around.

Hibiscus should be brought inside in late fall (the older the plant, the better it resists the cold) and left to overwinter in a bright but not-too-cool place. If hibiscus grows too bushy, it can be pruned back in the spring (like roses, see page 68). Prune young plants from time to time as this will make them grow more abundantly.

The plant doctor warns that scale insects and spider mites are attracted to hibiscus.

Umbrella plant

Loves to be in the wet

What it is:
• marsh-dweller with long stems and white flowers
• grows 2–3 feet tall
• perennial...
• ... but not hardy (zone 8)

What it needs:
• sunshine and warmth
• plenty of water; best to give it a long soak indoors in winter

Scientific name:
Cyperus involucratus

Your first duty to your umbrella plant is to soak it well. This marsh-dweller really flourishes when the lower part is wet and the upper part is warm and moist. The plant has long, elegant stems bearing long, narrow leaves arranged in the shape of an umbrella. It also grows small white flowers.

Depending on what you can afford, the umbrella plant is best bought as a small or large specimen ready for planting. Umbrella plants will grow up to 40 inches high and need loamy soil (see page 17). They love to soak in plenty of water. The plant can be put outdoors from the end of May, wrapped in some kind of all-round protection, or standing in a deep tray. The most important thing is always to give it sufficient water. Apart from that, a light feed every two weeks from June through September and a warm, sunny location are all it needs. Bring it indoors in winter, preferably into a warm, damp room, such as a bathroom. Spray it from time to time.

Stocks can be increased by cutting off the "umbrella" and about two inches of stem and sticking it upside down into damp sand or water. Plant it when it puts out roots.

99

Giant allium
Simply gigantic

What it is:
- hardy onion plant...
- ...with large mauve-pink flower balls
- stems grow up to 5 feet tall
- after flowering (June–July) the color is finished and the leaves fade

What it needs:
- sunshine
- regular watering ...
- ... but don't let the roots get waterlogged
- feeding once a week until it flowers
- cover the bulb and let it overwinter where it was planted (zone 8)

Scientific name:
Allium giganteum

The giant allium is simply enormous. Its stems grow up to 5 feet and bear mauve-pink flower balls (up to 10 inches in diameter). Plant the onions in the fall, preferably in large pots or borders or flower beds (you can also plant in early spring). Given sufficient sunshine and regular drinks of water, the giant allium will produce magnificent flowers in June–July. Until the flowering season, feed it once a week and don't allow the roots to get waterlogged.

The leaves fade immediately after flowering, so cut them off. The bulbs should be allowed to overwinter in the ground, covered with straw and twigs.

Styling Tip:
For an Asian look, arrange giant allium bulbs in geometric patterns — rows, squares, circles, or rectangles. Very stylish! Very authentic!

Kiwi fruit

Extremely decorative

What it is:
• climbing plant with heart-shaped leaves and fragrant flowers
• seldom bears fruit in cool growing zones
• hardy perennial (zone 4)

What it needs:
• semishade
• shelter
• a climbing support
• regular watering
• weekly feeding
• winter protection with straw and twigs in very cold zones

Scientific name:
Actinidia arguta

Kiwis — yes, of course we are familiar with them, they are the green egg-shaped fruits that you buy in the supermarket, hairy on the outside and deliciously sweet on the inside. If that's all you are interested in, skip this section!

Kiwis seldom fruit in the cooler growing zones, although (a short diversion into botany) it can be done through pollination. There are male and female kiwis, and one single male specimen is enough to pollinate 12 female kiwis, because only one male twig, in full bloom, is required for pollination to take place. Even if you follow all the rules and pollination takes place and real kiwi fruits grow, unfortunately they taste of nothing much. I have tried it myself. This doesn't matter however, because these exotic climbing plants are also incredibly attractive. They have heart-shaped, rich green leaves and the fragrant yellowish-white flowers bloom in May.

Buy kiwis as small plants (best to buy them in pairs) and plant them in pots or in the garden in late March or early April. What they really must have is something to help them climb (a wall with a trellis, a pergola, etc.), a sheltered semishaded location, and nutrient-rich, well-drained soil. Water them regularly and feed once a week in summer. In the fall, the kiwi foliage turns bright yellow.

Cover lightly with straw and twigs for the winter.

Mock strawberry

Climbs upward or hangs downward — well-suited for doing both

What it is:
• a graceful Asiatic perennial
• looks almost like a genuine strawberry, only more ornamental
• bears small red fruits, but they don't taste good
• not hardy (zone 6)

What it needs:
• semishade
• climbing support or hanging basket
• plenty of water
• weekly feeding
• bringing indoors in winter in colder zones

Scientific name:
Duchesnea indica

In some way the whole plant — leaves, flowers, and fruit — are reminiscent of the common strawberry family, but this plant looks more delicate, lacey, and tropical. Its small red fruits are quite pretty and are edible but don't have much flavor. Buy the mock strawberry as a small plant and put it outside in pots from the end of May. It needs a small trellis to help it to climb upward. You could also plant it in an aluminum bucket and attach it to the balcony railing, where it can show off its trailing elegance. It likes a semishaded location.

Water mock strawberry abundantly and regularly in summer and feed it once a week.

In winter, it must be brought indoors in cold zones, into a well-lit location that is not too warm, and should only be watered sparingly.

More mock strawberries can be obtained by division (pages 20–21).

Living stones

Stones that grow

What it is:
• flowers in the middle of the day...
• ...with two fleshy flattened leaves that look like stones
• from July through November it has glorious yellow or white flowers
• perennial, but not hardy (zone 9)

What it needs:
• sunshine
• sandy soil
• watering a little every 3–4 days from May through September...
• ...and feeding with cactus food once a month
• bringing indoors in winter in colder zones

Scientific name:
Lithops

Everyone knows the Rolling Stones. But the living stones are something else. In fact, they are not stones at all, but succulents that flower at midday and look like stones. The two fleshy leaves with a short underground stem make them hardly distinguishable from real stones. The living stones offer a special surprise from June through September, when beautiful yellow or white flowers appear between the two leaves.

Living stones can be found in the cactus and succulents section of nurseries. Very patient enthusiasts can also raise them themselves by sowing seeds in dishes containing sandy soil. Water them regularly and keep them warm. They should start to germinate after about six weeks. After six months, the small plants need two to three months rest without watering. Only then can they be planted in pots in sandy soil (or cactus compost) and placed outdoors.

Living stones, which come from the South African arid lands, require a sunny spot sheltered from the rain and can live on a balcony, patio, or in the garden. Water the living stones regularly in summer and feed with cactus food every 4 weeks. It is important to stop watering from September, at least until the old leaves have completely shriveled up. Only then should they be given a little water. You can't afford to fool around when watering the flowering stones. Too much puts them at risk of life and limb; in fact, they suffer a complete nervous breakdown!

The stones must be brought inside in winter to a bright, sunny spot that is not too warm. Stop watering them altogether.

Styling Tip:
Arrange living stones into a tableau with real stones.

Chusan palm

Absolutely essential tropical Basic

What it is:
• resistant potted palm...
• ...with a brown fibrous stem and lovely green palm leaves
• grows to a height of 60 feet
• perennial
• not hardy in cold growing zones (zone 9)

What it needs:
• semishade
• average but regular watering in summer
• feeding once a week until August
• bringing indoors in winter in colder zones

Scientific name:
Trachycarpus fortunei

With its brown fibrous palm stalk and deeply slit palm fronds, this is the absolute palm prototype. Its appearance immediately transports us into the realms of exoticism.

Buy the chusan palm as an established plant and plant it into the largest possible pot (this exotic tree can grow to 60 feet tall). Those who are brave enough and who live in growing zones in which the winter is not harsh can toughen it up in preparation for planting out in the garden. Chusan palms like a semishaded place. Young plants will not thrive in full sun

and they become prone to disease. In summer, the requirements are water regularly and feed once a week until August.

Potted palms must be wintered indoors in colder zones, either in a well-lit warm place or a cool dark place. It is essential that outdoor garden palms are well protected from the cold. The best method is to use wooden slats to build a "teepee" over the plant and then cover it loosely with plastic bubble wrap.

Devilwood

Fragrance of the East

What it is:
• evergreen shrub ...
• ... with small white clusters of flowers in July and August
• the flowers emit a provocative Eastern fragrance
• perennial, but not hardy (zones 5–6)

What it needs:
• semishade
• average but regular watering
• fertilizing once a month in summer
• bringing indoors in winter in colder zones

Scientific name:
Osmanthus x *burkwoodii*
Also known as osmanthus

These evergreen shrubs with dark green leathery leaves are laden from late June through August with small clusters of intensely fragrant white flowers.

Buy devilwood as a small plant and plant it in standard potting mixture in fairly large pots, tubs, or planters. From May onward it can be placed outdoors, preferably in semi-shade. Use an average amount of water on them but water regularly and feed every four weeks.

If overwintering devilwood in the house, stand it in a light, cool place.

Indian canna lily

As proud as an Indian rajah

What it is:
• summer-blooming rhizome ...
• ... with large green or red leaves ...
• ... and long stems with glorious white, yellow, orange, pink, and red blooms

What it needs:
• sunshine
• plenty of water
• fertilizing once a week
• overwintering in colder zones in a cool, dark peat-bed (zone 8)

Scientific name:
Canna indica hybrid

Indian canna lilies hail from the colorful world of maharajahs and come in all the colors of the rainbow — white, yellow, orange, pink, red, and even two-colored! The plants grow from 20 inches to 6 feet. They have large green or red leaves and long stems that bear glorious blooms from June through August.

Cannas are purchased as knobbly root systems known as rhizomes by the professionals. They should be planted in pots in March using standard potting mixture and placed on a sunny window sill inside the house. From mid to late May place the pot outdoors, in the border or flower bed or in a pot on the balcony. Make sure it is a sunny spot however. Water it every day (the soil should always be slightly moist), feed it once a week, and remove dead blooms regularly.

For the winter rest period, prepare the plant as follows: dig up the whole plant and cut it back to about 4 inches. Put the rhizomes in tubs, cover with dry peat, and keep in a cool, dark place until spring arrives.

Water Features

No evaporation

Don't let too much water evaporate from the mini-pond in summer, so the composition of the water remains balanced. Only add more water when necessary and never from the tap. Use standing water and use as little as possible. Clean the pond once a year and, at the same time, replace a quarter of the pond water with fresh water.

Ponds for all!

A pond on the third floor is possible, dear neighbor! Throw a handful of pond mixture into an old tin bathtub (standard potting mixture will do), and group plants together with netting around the roots to hold the soil and the roots together. Anchor them with stones so that they don't float to the surface. Fill with standing rainwater or water from the tap.

Water-lily trick

Small water-loving plants are also needed for the balcony pond, such as golden-yellow water forget-me-not (*Myosotis palustris*), the long, lilac iris (*Iris laevigata* 'Variegata'), and dwarf water lilies (*Nymphaea pygmaea*). Just in case the water lily doesn't flower, plastic ones look like the real thing. Go ahead, wing it.

A home pond

Can be created quite simply with an artificial pond or pond liner. Before they are dug in they are rather ugly but very practical. Place the pond at the bottom of the garden in the sun but not under the trees, in case too much foliage falls in and fouls the water. Protect young children from falling in.

Your own swamp

Plants for the garden pond: sweet grass (*Glyceria*), marsh marigold (*Caltha palustris*), arrowhead (*Saggitaria*). For the edge of the pond: white water lily (*Nymphaea* 'Virginalis') and frog's bit (*Hydrocharis morsus-ranae*). As floating plants; water violet, (*Hottonia palustris*) and water milfoil (*Myriophyllum*) as oxygen-producing plants underwater.

Fountains

Good taste is a duty, of course, when it comes to fountains. Yet until the image is ruined, you can live happily and without embarrassment. For those who revel in pure kitsch, buy an illuminated table-fountain (from hardware stores and garden centers), complete with high performance pump and hoses. Splish, splash!

Mud!

Children love mud and slop (they need it for their development – if you don't believe it, ask Freud). So set up a wonderful mud corner. Place a box of sand next to the hose tap or a large bucket of water and then (at least for a while) enjoy a few stress-free hours — until it's time to wash all those muddy clothes!

Water barrel

Rain water costs nothing, is low in lime content, is not as cold as tap water and, despite pollution, is most suitable for watering plants. Use wooden wine or whiskey barrels (from wineries or garden centers). A new metal or plastic one is fine, too.

Bird bath

Nature's operas with the dramatic twittering and trilling of arias can be heard at the bird bath especially at sunrise. There are two types of bird bath: flat stone dishes or those that come with their own stand. They may be made of cast iron or pottery. For the sake of economy, you could even use a saucer. The birds aren't worried either way!

Watering from below

More for the look than the genuine article but ideal for the job: water stones. They look and sound as if a gentle brook were babbling and splashing through your city garden. These are, in fact, specially bought stones with holes bored in them, with a circulating pump attached (from garden centers and by mail order).

Watering from above

The ultimate tip for hot days is to instal a shower outdoors. You can get various sizes from hardware and department stores. This is much better than showering indoors, as it's so wonderfully refreshing in summer. As an economical alternative, install a zinc watering can in a tree, and work the shower by pulling on a rope.

Gourme

First examine it, then eat it

t à la carte

At some time or other, someone gave me a few green leaves in a pot and tried to make me believe they'd produce wild strawberries.

Nice try! I thought. I would never have got the notion of creating a strawberry patch right on my fifth-floor balcony — crazy idea! Only expert fruit-growers could grow wild strawberries on a grand scale, maybe in woods... or anywhere but on a balcony, that's for sure.

Well, I had the greenery, so I watered, weeded, and well — I sort of did all of the things that have to be done. And one day, the pot was suddenly full of wild strawberries! Those tiny bright-red ones, as sweet as sugar. They looked good enough to eat!

That was a real no-brainer for me. Since then, I just stroll out onto the balcony, whenever I feel like fresh, green amaranth or tender arugula leaves to accompany pasta and pizza. Then there's the weirder stuff such as purple basil. You too can have all this even if you are a Basic Gardener with just a balcony—or any small patch of dirt.

Enjoyment without regret

Same old problem; you are a dedicated garlic lover, but unfortunately you are not a hermit. You won't be too popular if you reek of garlic during the morning office meeting!

The solution is bear's garlic (ramson or wild garlic). Minced or crushed, the leaves add a delicate flavor to soups, pasta sauces, salad dressings, and herb dips — without next day's smelly side-effects. Garlic grows best in shady, moist grass (look for the appropriate position in the yard or on your balcony), and the bright white flowers appear in early summer. The leaves should always be harvested before flowering.

For lateral gardeners I
Daisies

The weed that isn't, the common daisy (*Bellis perennis*) gives you a super-healthy kick in salads. It's robust, tough, hardy, and flowers almost all year round.

You can easily sow it out yourself. The whole plant is edible. The leaves taste a little like corn salad, the flowers have a slightly nutty, candied flavor (page 109), almost like marzipan. If you like the flavor, grow a patch of daisies for a continuous summer harvest.

If you feel it's a shame to eat these cute little flowers, try making a daisy chain or tying up a bracelet for your loved one — reverting to your childhood, so to speak. Wrapped in a damp towel, this work of art will keep fresh in the refrigerator for a couple of hours, but left outdoors, it will soon wilt.

Cooking Tip:
Serve daisy salad on its own or mixed with other flowers and leaves, or try crostini with tomato and daisies.

For lateral gardeners II
Sorrel

Grows wild in meadows and beside streams. It is also cultivated (in garden stores, ask for *Rumex acetosa*). Sorrel is hardy, and will last for four or five years.

Wherever you get it from, it tastes wonderfully sour, contains plenty of Vitamin C, and is ideal in herbal mixtures for salad dressings, dips, soups, and sandwich spread. In flower boxes, sorrel likes a shady position and plenty of water. You can buy it ready-planted in a pot or grow it yourself. It is best sown in the fall so it has time to overwinter, then you can harvest it for the table in spring and summer, and eat. Sorrel leaves also contain oxalic acid salts (not so healthy), so you should briefly blanch the leaves in boiling water before adding them to your recipe.

Cooking Tip:
For spring herb pesto with sorrel, crush or blend 1 cup each sorrel, basil, and arugula with $1/4$ cup each pumpkin seeds and grated pecorino cheese. Add 4 tablespoons each olive oil and lemon juice. Blend again and season with salt, pepper, and a pinch of sugar.

For lateral gardeners III
Dandelion

The poor dandelion is mercilessly persecuted and uprooted from grandpa's pristine lawn. But *Taraxacum officinale* is not only hardy, perennial, and undemanding, it is also a great salad ingredient, one that is extremely healthy.

The young leaves — rich in vitamins and minerals — have a slightly bitter flavor, but mixed with other kinds of salad greens, will liven up your salad bowl. The yellow flowers can be candied, or frozen into ice cubes as edible decorations for desserts and drinks.

Dandelion flowers can also be used as weather forecasters. They close before twilight if rain is on the way.

Ultra-conservative

Of course, fresh herbs will deteriorate with time. This is where preserving comes in. Herbs can be dried, pickled, or frozen.

Nice and dry
Robust herbs such as rosemary, thyme, and sage can be dried. Snip off whole sprigs, tie them loosely together, and hang them up to dry upside down in an airy place in your kitchen. Later, you can either leave them hanging like that as a decoration or strip the dried leaves from the stalks and store them in screw-top jars for cooking. They make great gifts for friends.

Nice and oily
The same sort of herbs can be preserved in vinegar. Put sprigs of herbs in bottles, fill up with white wine vinegar, and after 2 to 3 weeks you'll have herb vinegar. Soft young herb leaves, such as basil, can be preserved in olive oil. Use whole leaves and extra-virgin olive oil, pouring it into screw-top jars.

Nice and cool
Basil is suitable for freezing. Crush or mince the small leaves, and deep-freeze with a little water in ice trays, so you will have small portions when you need to defrost them for use.

Flower power!

You can do a lot more than just gaze dreamily at flowers. You can also enjoy eating them, drinking them, and using them as edible decorations.

Nasturtium, borage, sage, and daisy make very good eating, preferably in crispy salads. They are rich in vitamins, delicious in flavor, and a feast for the eyes.

Marigold and chamomile can be deep-frozen in ice cubes for dreamy summer drinks. Semi-freeze the flowers with a little water in ice trays. Fill the trays with water and re-freeze in the freezer compartment of the refrigerator for several hours.

Rose petals, whole violets, and violet petals can be candied and make classic decorations for cakes and desserts. This is how you do it: brush the petals with egg-white or gum arabic (obtainable from craft stores), roll in powdered sugar, and leave out to dry. Best to use home-grown flowers; they are guaranteed not to have been sprayed.

By the way, some people find it strange to eat flowers, despite all the vitamins they contain, and really have to force themselves to take a bite. It's a matter of personal preference. Flowers can always be used as decoration.

Redcurrant

Lots of vitamins to keep you healthy!

What it is:
• a hardy bush (zones 5–6) whose berries are red (slightly sour), white (a little sweeter), or black (sweetest)
• harvested in mid-summer
• grows up to 5 feet high
• can be standard or espaliered

What it needs:
• sun to partial shade
• plenty of moisture
• feeding every 8 weeks until August

Scientific names:
Ribes rubrum (red- and white- currant),
Ribes nigrum (black currant)

Top with sugar and cream, and enjoy these delicious summer fruits. Or transform them into a juicy fruit flan. Or make the currants into a fruit juice. Or eat them straight from the bush. They are all good eating, and just 1 cup of black currants will give you double the daily requirements of Vitamin C.

When you buy a currant bush, it needn't have more than 5 to 10 shoots, but make sure the bush will bear berries. Ask in the store whether it is "self-pollinating," as some black currants, for instance, are not. Plant out in fall or very early spring. Don't plant them too close to each other. They need a space of 5–6 feet between them to fully spread out. Currants like a sunny position best, but partial shade is also okay. Always provide sufficient moisture and long term fertilizer in spring (page 25). Apply it every 8 weeks until August.

To ensure an abundant harvest, prune rigorously. Begin just after planting, leaving only the strongest, widely spaced shoots, and cut these down to a third. Be radical! Cut out the older shoots after harvesting and in winter. After you have had the bushes a few years, prune all the shoots older than 4 years right to the ground. Leave up to 12 shoots standing. That will give the bush some air.

Bushes grown on balconies may need frost protection in colder zones (pages 30–31).

The reason these fruits are not well-known in the United States is that they are prone to a fungal parasite that also attacks white fir and can ruin forests. Check with your local garden center if it is okay to grow them.

Blackberry

Velvety, sweet & juicy

What it is:
• perennial climber, with black, shiny berries ripening in late summer/early fall
• hardy (zone 6)

What it needs:
• lots of sun, preferably on south-facing walls
• watering regularly
• fertilizing once a season
• wrapping up warm in winter (in colder zones)

Scientific name:
Rubus fruticosus
Suggested variety: 'Black Satin' – no thorns!

Blackberries like sunny, sheltered positions, so they can be espaliered on south-facing walls. Tie the tendrils loosely with raffia.

It's best to buy a tiny blackberry bush in a pot and plant it out in spring. Fertilize immediately with organic fertilizer (page 25) and, depending on the variety, you will have white, pink, or red flowers from late June and big, black, juicy berries from late summer through fall.

Blackberries are sensitive to cold but will survive if well covered with straw. Don't remove the slightly rotting straw next spring — blackberries love a mulch!

Quince

Delicious jellies and pre-serves from your own tree

What it is:
• small tree or bush, 6–18 ft high
• self-pollinating
• attractive, pale pink flowers
• delicious fruit from mid-October (once it is cooked through)
• hardy (zone 4)

What it needs:
• a sunny position
• shelter from the wind
• fairly light soil

Scientific name:
Cydonia oblonga

Suggested variety: 'Champion', needs little care and produces lots of fruit.

Quince varies a lot in appearance, from resembling a slightly downy yellow apple to the red and green pear-shaped variety shown here. Unlike the quince's distant relatives, apples and pears, it cannot be eaten right off the tree. Raw quince flesh is incredibly tough and grainy and pretty flavorless. When cooked it turns a lovely pink color and can be made into the most delicious jams, jellies, and preserves.

Harvesting quince is really Basic: quince are self-pollinating and, unlike many other kinds of fruit, often fruit singly.

Quince comes as a bush or small tree. The quince is hardy, needs a light soil, and almost never gets diseases. All it needs is a sunny position, sheltered from the wind. The flowers can be white or pink. The fruit ripens in mid-fall.

Perhaps the best thing about quince is that given suitable protection from wind and from too much sun in desert regions, it will grow throughout the United States and Canada.

Cooking Tip:
Quince are delicious candied or cooked, puréed, and mixed with an equal amount of sugar, then spread out thinly to dry. This quince paste candy is a Middle Eastern favorite.

Amaranth

Very healthy. Very fashionable. And on top of that, really easy to grow!

What it is:
• fast-growing annual
• grows up to 40 inches high
• hardy and undemanding
• delicious leaves prepared like spinach

What it needs:
• watering daily
• fertilizer once a week

Scientific name:
Amaranthus mangostanus

This exotic plant with large green leaves can be found on menus in places as far apart as China, South America, India, Africa, and Mexico. The Incas grew amaranth and it was, and still is, a favorite dish among native Americans. It is very similar to spinach in texture and flavor; hence its popularity everywhere but Europe. Non-native Americans discovered amaranth late, so it is still something of a novelty.

Amaranth is actually much healthier than spinach. It has the highest iron content of all green leafy vegetables, huge amounts of vitamin C, and even amino acids (good for the brain and nervous system). UNICEF calls amaranth "the manna of the third millennium" because its seeds have the potential to make a major contribution to the world fight against famine.

There are around 1,200 varieties of amaranth! *A. mangostanus* is quite hardy and will tolerate a slight drop in temperature.

Sowing: order the seeds from mail-order suppliers and sow in rows of around 15 inches apart in late April/early May. If the plants grow too close together, plant further apart later. Water daily and fertilize once a week.

Cooking Tip:

The leaves make a great cooked vegetable to eat with broiled fish or meat. Sauté some green onions and chili pepper rings in a little oil. Add raw or briefly blanched amaranth leaves. Season with salt, cayenne pepper, and lime juice — and keep your guests guessing!

Strawberry spinach

The "all-in-one" vegetable

What it is:
• looks like anything but spinach
• ornamental annual fruit and vegetable
• small leaves that look like arugula
• fruits that look like raspberries but...
• ...have a strawberry flavor

What it needs:
• a sunny position
• watering regularly
• fertilizer once a week

Scientific name:
Chenopodium capitatum

Strawberry spinach is not a spinach at all, but a relative of quinoa and goosefoot. The leaves look like those of arugula and can be stewed, steamed, or used raw in mixed salads. The red fruits look a little like raspberries, but taste more like strawberries.

This delicious vegetable/fruit can't be found in the stores, but it is available through mail order. Start it in small pots on a sunny window sill from March, then plant out the seedlings in planters or flower beds in late May. It needs plenty of sun, regular watering, and a little fertilizer once a week.

Pak choi

A taste of the Orient!

What it is:
- Chinese cabbage
- easy to grow and fast to pick
- full-flavored, peppery taste
- great in salads, perfect as a wok vegetable

What it needs:
- sunshine
- regular watering

Scientific name:
Brassica rapa

Pak choi has white, wide, crispy stalks and dark green, shiny leaves, both of which are completely edible. It has a spicy, slightly peppery flavor. The name pak choi is Chinese and means "mustard greens". It is related to Chinese cabbage but looks and tastes more like Swiss chard. Pak choi is a great salad green and is good in a Chinese-style stirfry!

The best thing about this versatile vegetable is that it's so easy to grow! Let the seeds sprout on a sunny window sill in early spring, and plant out the seedlings 16 inches apart from mid-May. Pak choi can reach a height of 15–20 inches. Water regularly and every 2–3 weeks, fertilize. Give it another 2 or 3 months and harvest.

Strawberry

Pick wild strawberries on your own balcony!

What it is:
- dreamily delicious fruit
- rich in vitamin C but low in calories
- fruits in early summer (earlier in California)
- pretty as an evergreen, hardy ground-cover

What it needs:
- sunshine
- a little protection in winter in colder zones (zone 5)

Scientific name:
Fragaria varieties

Everyone loves strawberries! That's why there are so many different varieties and cultivars. There is a variety of alpine strawberry that keeps producing fruits all through summer. The great favorite, however, is the tiny wild strawberry, with its delicious taste and dizzying fragrance. Despite the delicacy of its delicious fruits, the strawberry is quite a hardy plant.

Alpine strawberries:
Sow the seeds in April. Keep the seedlings in the shade and make sure they have plenty of moisture. Then thin them out until they are planted 2 inches apart and, after the last frost, they can be put outdoors in flower beds (or buy them ready-planted in a strawberry pot). Harvest the berries from June through fall. When fruiting is finished, cut back the foliage and provide light winter protection with twigs.

Wild strawberries:
If you are lucky enough to live near a wood where they grow, take cuttings from one or two runners, plant them in your garden, and give them plenty of water. If you grow them on the balcony, the planter should be wide and shallow. Otherwise, you can buy them by mail order.

Cultivated varieties:
Buy young plants and initially plant out in a row. They quickly grow into a healthy evergreen even with minimum care. They grow in any soil and make excellent ground-cover for beneath trees. And the best of all: harvest for up to five years without a great deal of work.

Cooking Tips:
Purée strawberries with cream cheese, a little powdered sugar, and a dash of almond liqueur. Or marinate whole berries with balsamic vinegar and icing sugar for 1 to 2 hours.

Borage

An absolutely uncompli-
cated type. Try getting
to know it.

What it is:
• annual herb with pretty blue flowers ...
• ... and tasty leaves
• tastes and smells like cucumber

What it needs:
• sun to partial shade
• lots of fertilizer
• lots of room

Scientific name:
Borago officinalis

Okay, so maybe its fairly long, downy leaves
don't look that exciting. But we gourmets
know better! The delightful, slightly sour,
cucumber flavor of borage leaves is the perfect
salad ingredient. The herb also has its pretty
blue, star-shaped flowers to offer. They taste
as good as they look.

Buy 1 or 2 borage plants in the spring. Plant
them 12–20 inches apart, because borage
needs a lot of space. It grows to a height of
2 to 3 feet. It's undemanding and even thrives
in the shade. However, it needs a good feed
every so often; use organic fertilizer. Borage

only lives for one summer. Pick only the
young, velvety-soft leaves. Chop or grind them
and add them to salad dressings, dips,
sauces, and spreads. The flowers make
attractive decorations for salads or other
dishes. Or try adding a handful to white wine
vinegar and sealing in jars. Leave for a few
days, then amaze your dinner guests by
putting blue vinegar on the table!

The plant doctor says: although borage
attracts bees and bumblebees, it also
attracts aphids. The only solution is constant
monitoring, spraying, and wiping the leaves.
Remove heavily infested flowers and stalks.

Sweet woodruff

Flowers for the punch bowl

What it is:
• perennial herb (zone 5)
• grows only six inches high
• flowers in May and June
• its bewitching fragrance ...
• ... has an intoxicating effect

What it needs:
• a shady to dark location
• damp soil

Scientific name:
Galium odoratum

As a woodland plant, sweet woodruff
obviously grows best in the undergrowth,
where the soil is damp and shady. When it
thrives, it puts out runners which will carpet
the garden. The star-shaped leaves make it
attractive ground-cover. Sweet woodruff
was once grown for its medicinal properties,
but the Germans use it to flavor a punch
called *Maibowle*.

Sweet woodruff should be bought as a plant
in fall or early spring. Plant it out at 10-inch
intervals. If sweet woodruff is to thrive, it
needs a woodland atmosphere in your
garden, a section that is damp and shady.

The small white fragrant flowers appear in
early summer. It is only when they start to
wilt that the typical woodruff fragrance of
new-mown hay develops. Cut off stalks with
flowers, then leave them to dry.

The best use for sweet woodruff is to dry it
and mix it with other dried grasses and seed
heads, so that it imparts a lovely fragrance
to the room.

Garlic chive

Great for soups and sauces

What it is:
• looks like chives
• tastes like garlic
• the leaves have less odor than garlic
• perennial (zone 3)

What it needs:
• partial shade
• loamy soil, rich in humus
• regular watering

Scientific name:
Allium tuberosum

This is the Asian cousin of garlic and chives. It looks more like chives, since the leaves and/or stalks are grass-like and flat. The smell and taste are more reminiscent of garlic, but more delicate and subtle. Not only the leaves and stalks are edible, but so are the flowers when in bud.

Sow garlic chives from late March. The plants grow from seed to 10–20 inches high in 3–4 months. They can also be bought in pots; a more practical solution that ensures that they are ready for eating at an earlier stage. Like most herbs, garlic chives like a warm, sunny, bright location, though partial shade is also okay, and they prefer a loamy, rich soil. Water regularly.

Use snipped or minced garlic chives to season Chinese or Thai food, or use instead of garlic in soups, sauces, and dressings. Since garlic chives are milder than garlic cloves, you can enjoy the garlic flavor without inflicting it on anyone else.

Styling tip:
Whole stalks of garlic chives make an attractive decoration for salads, appetizers, etc.

Lovage

A tasty secret!

What it is:
• perennial growing to 6 feet in height
• less expansive in a pot
• can last for fifteen years or more
• long stalks with large, feathery leaves
• full-flavored and hardy (zone 4)
• likes shade and bees

What it needs:
• full sun to full shade
• very damp soil
• fertilize once a year
• light winter protection in cold zones

Scientific name:
Levisticum officinale

Buy lovage in spring as a seedling. If you plant it out in the yard, if you're lucky, it will grow into a bush six feet high, though it is unlikely to live beyond 15 years. On the balcony, however, it usually manages to live for only two or three years and doesn't grow very tall.

Other tricks to growing lovage are always to keep the soil slightly moist, fertilize it once a season, and cover lightly with twigs and straw in winter. In summer, lovage produces pale yellow umbelliferous flowers that are favorites with the bees.

Perhaps the most interesting fact about lovage is that it is reputed to have an aphrodisiac effect. But that is a separate research project for each intrepid gardener...

Salad burnet

Delicious in a herb sauce

What it is:
- hardy, undemanding herb (zone 2)
- spherical green buds, producing tiny red flowers
- and fine green leaves — delicious with a French dressing
- also known as lesser burnet

What it needs:
- sunshine and warmth
- that's all there is to it

Scientific name:
Sanguisorba minor

Salad burnet grows to about 18 inches high and is a herb that has gone out of fashion for no good reason. Good news for gourmets is that this herb with long-stemmed, slightly jagged, pale green, thin leaves has been rediscovered.

Salad burnet can be bought as a small plant at well-stocked nurseries and sometimes in farmers' markets. If you grow it from seed, sow in late March, then thin out the seedlings, leaving 8–12 inches between them.

Salad burnet thrives in soil that is not too damp, and in a sunny and warm location. The small, round, greenish buds and its leaves taste wonderfully fresh, slightly bitter, nutty, with a hint of cucumber. Keep dead-heading flowers, which will result in an even more abundant crop.

For the best flavor, the leaves should be chopped, and a little lemon juice and olive oil added.

Salad burnet was introduced into the U.S. by the first settlers from Europe, where it had been used as a medicinal herb.

Cooking Tips:

Herb Sauce: mince half a cup each of parsley, borage, salad burnet, tarragon, and chervil leaves, and add a bunch of minced chives. Add 3 tablespoons each of mayonnaise and yogurt and two finely chopped hard-cooked eggs. Season with lemon juice, mustard, salt, and pepper.

Golden purslane

The gourmet's delight!

What it is:
- annual herb, grows to 4 to 5 inches high
- another herb used by top chefs

What it needs:
- sunshine
- regular watering
- well-drained soil

Scientific name:
Portulaca okracea sativa

Rediscovered by top chefs, golden purslane is enjoying a comeback these days. The leaves taste slightly sour and salty, so it add zing to salads, herbal dips, herb soups, or vegetables braised in butter.

Visually, the leaves look like the foliage of a miniature rubber plant, being fleshy and shiny green. Golden purslane is an annual. The seeds were once given to children as a vermifuge.

It's best to grow golden purslane from seed Sow the tiny seeds from mid- to late May

directly into flower boxes or beds, around 6 to 8 inches apart, or plant as seedlings in pots on your window sill in April.

Golden purslane can't bear the cold, and does best in locations in which the sun shines all day. Water sparingly but regularly. Whatever you do, avoid waterlogged soil!

Cooking Tip:

Golden purslane leaves are delicious with London broil or rib of beef, sliced paper-thin. Or try them mixed with fresh wild mushrooms and tossed in a lemon vinaigrette. To make cream of golden purslane soup, lightly sauté in butter 1 cup golden purslane leaves with 2 minced shallots and 1 crushed garlic clove. Add 1 cup vegetable broth and simmer for 6-8 minutes. Transfer to a food-processor or blender and blend well. Add $1/2$ cup light cream and mix well. Return to the pot briefly to reheat. Season with salt, pepper, and nutmeg to taste. Pour into individual bowls and top with 1 table-spoon thick plain yogurt just before serving. Garnish with golden purslane leaves.

Arugula

Simply the best — with almost everything

What it is:
• super-fast grower in a planter or in a flower bed ...
• ... taking only 3–4 weeks before it is ready for picking
• full-flavored, nutty, astringent flavor

What it needs:
• lots of sunshine
• lots of warmth
• lots of water
• sow the seeds several times a season

Scientific name:
Eruca sativa

The arugula fan club is expanding daily. There are people who are absolutely crazy about its fresh, rich salad flavor. The long, ragged leaves have a spicy flavor, tasting like a combination of nutmeg, black pepper, and mustard. Although arugula has become fashionable in gourmet kitchens, it is no newcomer to the food scene. In fact, it has been a regular feature of the Middle Eastern diet for more than 2,000 years.

Here is the quickest way to home-grown arugula salad. Plant the seeds in flower boxes or beds. As little as 3–4 weeks later you will be able to pick delicious, fresh vita-mins. The trick is not to plant the seeds too close together. Choose a sunny location, and water plentifully and regularly. You can keep planting seeds until the fall, to ensure that arugula becomes a regular ingredient in your salad bowl.

Cooking Tip:

Arugula can be used in almost any savory dish, including salads, soups, pasta, and sauces, though the strong flavor means it needs to be mixed with other greens and used sparingly. For example, combine whole arugula leaves, halved cherry tomatoes, and shavings of good-quality parmesan, then toss with cold pasta — a summer hit! Or create a completely new kind of pesto sauce in the blender or food-processor by combining arugula, sunflower seeds, pecorino, and garlic. Or pep up a regular frozen pizza with an arugula topping. Or sauté arugula leaves in olive oil, and sprinkle with salt, pepper, and lemon juice. Buon appetito!

Purple basil

The king of herbs to crown your best dishes

What it is:
• annual herb ...
• ... with purple leaves, fragrant aroma, and sweet, peppery flavor

What it needs:
• sunshine
• dry, sandy soil
• frost-free location

Scientific name:
Ocimum basilicum purpurascens

This is the somewhat eccentric brother of the sweet basil. Like its green relative purple basil is aromatic with sweetish but peppery flavor. The whole plant is a deep purple color, with large shiny leaves—a truly royal herb.

Buy basil seedlings in the spring, and don't plant them out until there's no chance of even a slight ground frost at night. Basil needs dry, sandy soil and a sunny, sheltered location. This is true of all varieties, green and purple.

Harvest the larger, lower leaves, which can be eaten raw and whole, minced, or ground in salad dressings, pasta dishes, and pizza.

Cooking Tip:

Here's something that you won't find at a restaurant — basil sauce as a dessert! Purèe the leaves, press the purèe through a fine sieve, and combine with icing sugar and lime juice. Yummy with berries and vanilla ice-cream!

Coriander (Cilantro)

Not just for Mexican food

What it is:
• annual herb ...
• ... with filigree leaves on delicate stems
• pale pink umbelliferous flowers, turning into small round seed capsules
• as important in Asian cooking as it is in Mexican

What it needs:
• sunshine
• daily watering
• complete shelter from the wind

Scientific name:
Coriandrum sativum

Another name for cilantro is Chinese parsley, and as that indicates, it is as important a herb in Chinese cooking (as well as Indian) as it is in Mexican. Some people love the spicy, lemony, slightly "burnt" flavor, others hate it. But if you like it, why not try growing it at home?

Coriander (cilantro) has feathery, green leaves on delicate stalks, looking very much like its close relative, flat-leaved parsley. It flowers in high summer, producing pale pink umbels, which turn into small round seed capsules.

You can buy coriander (cilantro) as a plant, but it is just as easy to sow the seeds straight into boxes, pots, or flower beds. Sow them in the spring. It needs a sunny and, above all, sheltered location and needs regular watering. In hot climates and in summer, water it daily.

Cilantro is eaten as a fresh herb, chopped or minced and combined with a whole host of Mexican, Chinese, Indian, and Thai dishes, including noodles and exotic salads. Coriander seeds, finely crushed in a mortar, are used in curry pastes and to flavor the sauce for couscous.

Lemon balm

For your favorite cakes and cookies and "is there any left?" desserts

What it is:
• perennial, hardy herb (zone 2)
• spreads rapidly
• smells and tastes lemony
• hypnotic qualities loved by bees
• dessert compatible

What it needs:
• a sheltered location
• plenty of water

Scientific name:
Melissa officinalis

If you like lemons, lemon balm will be a feast for your senses. It is one of the few herbs that goes as well with savory as with sweet dishes including cakes and desserts. It is a favorite ingredient in long drinks, such as shrub and claret cup. Lemon balm has a fresh, clean flavor, and makes a tempting decoration for fancy cakes and cookies. The leaves are pale green and heart-shaped. Rub them between your fingers, and you will immediately smell that pleasant lemony fragrance.

It's best to buy lemon balm as a small seedling. In a sheltered location, lemon balm will feel so much at home that it will spread like wildfire. The only solution is a "surgical" root reduction in late fall. Give it plenty of water in summer, and in winter cover it with a twig mulch. It may need organic fertilizer once a season (page 25).

Always use lemon balm leaves raw, as they lose their flavor when cooked. Lemon balm has an intoxicating effect on bees, which is why another old English name for it is bee-balm.

Wheat grass

As basic as chives

What it is:
• the healthiest grass in the world
• fantastic in salads, sauces, and on bread
• easy to grow

What it needs:
• sunshine
• plenty of water
• that's all there is to it

Scientific name:
Triticum aestivum

Wheat grass has been a favorite ingredient in expensive health drinks served in juice bars, so why not save some money and boost your health by enjoying wheat grass at home? Apart from squeezing the juice or adding it to other vegetables in the blender, it can be chopped or minced and added to salads, sauces, and even sprinkled on bread. Plant wheat sprouts in a pot or tub, place in a warm, sunny location, water regularly, and always keep slightly moist. It won't take long for the wheat grass to send up shoots.

The vitamin values peak when the wheat is 1–2 weeks old. You can keep planting the wheat seeds – indoors in winter, outdoors in summer – and you'll have a non-stop supply of super-healthy "life-food"!

Basic Tip:
Good news for the health and fitness fanatics who are too lazy to grow wheat – get your health out of a bottle! You can now get wheat grass concentrate in powder form from health food stores.

Chamomile

Herb teas for the Basic Gardener

What it is:
- undemanding annual 8 to 20 inches tall
- exceptionally easy to grow
- flowers after only 6–8 weeks
- distinctive fragrance
- make home-made chamomile tea from the dried flowers

What it needs:
- plenty of sunshine
- moderate watering
- and that's all there is to it

Scientific name:
Matricaria recutita

As soon as colds and flu strike, it's time to start making chamomile tea. (There is also a perennial chamomile, *Chamaemelum nobile*.)

Annual chamomile is real easy to grow. Honestly! Best plant the tiny seeds mixed with a little sand straight into flower beds or planters from March onward, leaving a space of 8–12 inches between them, and water generously.

If chamomile gets enough sun (the more sun, the stronger its healing powers), it will begin flowering as soon as 6 – 8 weeks after planting. The white flowers, that look like daisies with bulbous yellower centers, are the important part. They should be picked 3–5 days after coming into bloom, then laid out to dry, and stored, in a hermetically sealed container in a dark place (use brown glass screw-top jars).

To make the tea add half a cupful of flowers to a teapot, then add boiling water and leave the tea to steep for about five minutes. Drink it piping hot.

What goes with it:
True chamomile can be planted among cabbage, potatoes, and leeks.

Basic Tip:
Chamomile stands for patience, gentleness, and modesty. But really, with those qualities, it needn't be so modest. An infusion of its flowers is not only enjoyable as tea, it's also great as a steam bath for facial cleansing. Cooled down and strained, a chamomile decoction is the ideal hair rinse for organic blondes.

Hyssop

Medication for eyes and stomach

What it is:
- hardy, undemanding perennial (zone 2)
- grows up to 40 inches in height
- ... with an aromatic fragrance and astringent taste ...
- flowers in decorative blue spikes

What it needs:
- sunshine
- a large container
- daily watering

Scientific name:
Hyssopus officinalis

Hyssop has a strong aromatic fragrance. The flavor is rather astringent and slightly bitter. Salads, dips, potatoes, and vegetable dishes can be spiced up with a little hyssop. Your digestive system will thank you and it is also good for the eyesight. But hyssop is also a feast for the eyes with its many small, bright blue flowers, which grow on long spikes. This herb can grow up to 40 inches and has narrow, pointed, tough green leaves.

Hyssop is well-suited for growing at home. Plant the seeds in little pots in March/April and leave them to germinate on a sunny

window sill; in May, the seedlings can be replanted in the open air. Leave 12 inches between the seedlings. For hyssop to thrive it needs sunshine. If it lives in a pot, it needs plenty of growing space for the roots and requires daily watering in the heat. Pick it throughout the summer.

Hyssop propagates very well from cuttings (pages 20–21).

In cooking, it is best to mix hyssop with other herbs.

All the garden pests, such as slugs and caterpillars, hate hyssop, and beat a hasty retreat from it.

Cooking Tip:
Hyssop vinegar and hyssop oil:Finely mash around 3 handfuls of hyssop leaves with 4 tablespoons of white wine vinegar or with 4 tablespoons of olive oil. Press this purèe through a fine sieve, top up with white wine vinegar or olive oil in a bottle.

Peppermint

Multipurpose herb for beginners

What it is:
• a rampant hardy perennial
• eaten fresh — a delicious seasoning
• used dry — a sprinkling herb or herb tea

What it needs:
• full sun
• dry soil

Scientific name:
Mentha x *piperita*

Peppermint is a herb that grows beside water in the wild. As a seasoning, fresh mint leaves are delicious in sauces and in a sauce, British-style, with lamb or mutton. The dried herb is drunk as a health-giving tea and sprinkled on yogurt as a seasoning.

As far as mint varieties go, you are spoiled for choice. In addition to peppermint, there is orange and pineapple mint, apple mint, Moroccan mint, spearmint —the list is endless.

It's best to buy ready-grown plants in pots, then plant it out in spring. In the garden, all varieties of mint like dry soil and full sun. If the mint is doing well, it will happily spread

in all directions. You can cut it back, but using it as ground cover will certainly deter the weeds.

Fresh leaves can be picked throughout the summer. The main time for harvesting is in June, shortly before flowering. This is the time to cut most herbs down to the ground. Then tie them in bunches and hang them upside down to dry. Mint may produce a second harvest in late summer. In winter, the plant dies back completely but re-emerges in spring. It needs hardly any tending.

What goes with it:
Don't put mint and chamomile together, but mint enjoys the proximity of tomatoes and lettuce.

Cooking Tip:
Why not try mint jelly? You can eat it with any meat, not just lamb. Bring $2^{1}/_{4}$ cups of good clear apple juice to boil with 1 cup sugar. Add 2 sprigs of fresh mint. Pour into a screw-top jar. Add more mint leaves or sprigs. Seal tightly and leave to set in a cool place.

Tomato

This one is striped!

What it is:
- tall bush or vine grown as an annual ...
- bearing the famous bright red fruit
- pick from July through October
- bushes can grow as high as 3 feet
- easy to grow yourself
- super-healthy
- unpopular with mosquitoes

What it needs:
- plenty of sunshine
- watering up to twice daily
- liquid feed once a week
- absolutely frost-free environment

Scientific name:
Lycopersicon esculentum

Suggested variety: our favorite variety is red with yellow stripes (pictured above).

The first tomatoes to migrate from South America did so when the Aztecs still had an empire, in the 16th century. They weren't red at all, they were yellow! And they weren't considered edible, but grown as ornamental plants. They were all gussied up in their Sunday best in the ornamental gardens of the European nobility. This tomatoless period of deprivation lasted for fifty years. It isn't so surprising, as the tomato comes from a family of plants whose European varieties are poisonous. Then came the breakthrough, and since then, this delicious red fruit has become commonplace on plates throughout the world. Strange to think that the mainstay of Italian cuisine was unknown to the Romans! The tomato is rich in vitamins and low in calories.

In cooler growing zones, tomatoes are annual, but in their native land they are perennials.

Plant the seeds in late March/early April in pots on a sunny window sill. Prick out the seedlings when they are 6–8 inches high, and space them at least 16 inches apart in pots or flower beds in mid to late May (or when you can be sure there will be no more ground frost). Or buy plants ready-grown.

Tomatoes like it hot, that's why they like locations in front of white reflecting house walls. Dig them in as deep as possible (up to where the leaves start growing). This encourages them to put out side roots, making them stronger.

Always give tomatoes plenty of water. If it gets really hot in summer, potted tomatoes may need two waterings, morning and evening. They need one feed a week. You should be able to enjoy a continuous harvest from July through late October, and these tomatoes have a flavor that is so much better than those in the supermarket!

Varieties suitable for the balcony are 'Tiny Tim' and 'Minibel' dwarf cherry tomato.

The name tomato is derived from the Mexican *tomatl*, which means "bad odor." The dark green, ragged leaves do indeed give off an unpleasant smell that makes mosquitoes back off. So, in summer, leave a tomato twig on your bedside table at night!

Cooking Tip:
Summer's health drink for tomato lovers: Chop 4 large tomatoes coarsely, then blend in a food-processor and push through a sieve. Combine with $1/2$ cup each of freshly squeezed orange and grapefruit juices. Add a pinch of herb salt and 1-2 splashes of Tabasco, and serve ice-cold with a sprig of mint or lemon balm for garnish.

Indian corn

Delicious with herb butter

What it is:
• yellow, dark red, purple, white, and blue-black corn cobs
• pick in August/September
• needs a lot of space; best grown in beds

What it needs:
• regular watering
• feeding once a week

Scientific name:
Zea mays

Suggested variety: 'Tom Thumb' popcorn maize, a dwarf variety suitable for small gardens. When dried you can make popcorn.

Indian corn looks as if it has been painted: yellow, dark red, white, and blue-black corn; sometimes a cob contains a mixture of colors. And it's a classic, pre-Columbian native American vegetable.

For growing at home, plant 2 to 3 corn seeds into a seed-hole from mid to late May, preferably not in rows, but in a square (best for its pollination habit). Corn is more suitable for a garden or yard, as it needs a lot of space. Water regularly, and feed once a week.

Or you could copy the Native American trick of simply adding a fish head to each seed-hole as you plant the corn!

In late summer (late August/ early September) the corn will be ripe. This is when the golden yellow corn-silk starts turning brown inside the husk and the cobs are fat and round. Boil corn-on-the-cob for 5 minutes in salted water, then sauté it in herb butter. Or cook it on the barbecue.

Eggplant

The versatile vegetable

What it is:
• purple vegetable
• grows to a height of 32 inches
• ready to pick in August
• steamed or baked it has few calories and tastes very good

What it needs:
• lots of sunshine and warmth
• regular watering

Scientific name:
Solanum melongena

Synonyms: aubergine, garden egg
Suggested variety: 'White Eggplant', a dwarf variety with small fruits, the ideal balcony vegetable (available by mail-order).

Eggplants like a south-facing location. If you have a greenhouse, that is even better because, if at all possible, eggplant are even greater sun-worshippers than tomatoes. If you can't offer them such a life of luxury, then better not grow them, because instead of long, fat eggplants around 12 inches long, you'll end up with puny, stunted fruits, if the plant bothers to produce fruit at all.

You can buy dwarf varieties for your balcony, which are more suited to life in a tub. The smaller, white eggplants, for example, called garden eggs in Africa, are ideal for tubs. Although the white eggplants look just like eggs, they grow in clusters and have nothing to do with chickens. They taste like their larger relatives and, all in all, they look quite pretty if you like something special.

Start the seeds in a container in a very warm, sunny position (next to the radiator in a cold climate) from mid to late March. The small plants can be planted out 16 inches apart from late May or even June unless it's really hot. When they have taken root, cut off all but 3 or 4 of the tendrils because then you'll have less green and more fruits.

Eggplants need a lot of sun and warmth. So, if you live in a cool growing zone and get a cold spell in the summer or long periods of rain, bring the plants indoors. Eggplants need daily watering and feeding once a week with an organic fertilizer.

The t

If I have to grin and bear it, so should my plants

ugh
guys

Plants are like people; some are tough and when they come through for you they win your respect and give you a sense of achievement.

Let's take balcony plants. They live in the inner city, beside busy roads, and may not have more than 4 inches of dirt in which to live. They are sometimes exposed to the full force of rainstorms without protection or shelter.

These rugged conditions are not for every plant, and many succumb. I have been experimenting for years with growing plants on the balcony and only the hardiest have survived.

But it was worth it, because the first thing I see every morning through the windows of my city center apartment is tender green shoots — no concrete.

How "tough" is tough?

The stench of automobiles is everywhere. In many inner cities, more than 50% of the trees are in poor health because of exhaust emissions. In spite of this, I still use the balcony (granted, it's not exactly next to a freeway on-ramp, but there are still plenty of car fumes around). And, despite the pollution, I still like sitting outside. So naturally, I have to have plants that can cope with the traffic at least as well as I can.

And they do exist! Cherry laurel, for example, or plectranthus. When you buy them, look at the plastic tag in the pot. It will tell you whether the plant can withstand pollution. This is no fantasy-word but a highly scientific label, a cast-iron guarantee that the plants will still look good in the innermost inner-city area. Incidentally, this label isn't just added at random; it is the result of constant testing conducted by universities and research institutions. The plants that have passed the test in years of Basic Gardening experiments are plectranthus, sunflower, nasturtium, sweet pea, and catmint.

I used to be a gutter

The ultimate test for toughness is to use old aluminum guttering or siding as a plant container for city window sills. It can be nailed to the window frame quite easily with roofing felt nails (and it's bomb- and storm-proof!). It doesn't care what the weather is like. It never rusts, weathers, sheers, or snaps. Although it's shallow and there's not much room for soil and no drainage holes, many plants will happily take to it — for example, nasturtiums.

Aristocratic and elegant

Topiary work, using box bushes or hedges, has been around a long time. It was in fashion in ancient Rome and was revived in the sixteenth century. Under the shears of the English and the French, with their sense of royal style à la Versailles or Windsor, box became something quite prestigious. Nowadays, any florist worthy of the name has a large box sculpture on display in the window.

Do-it-yourself box styling is also back in fashion. Why not try it yourself? All you need is a luxuriant box bush and you can snip away at it with the secateurs creating whatever shape you fancy. Don't buy a dwarf variety; box grows very slowly (which is why it is so expensive). One or two light prunings a year should suffice; if possible, early in the year and in early summer. In the South and West, bay-trees work just as well.

Then you will need a basic wire framework. You can fashion creative ones yourself or buy standard ones ready-made. Place the wire frame over the plant and cut away anything that tries to grow out through it. Use shears for ambitious projects and secateurs for miniature works of art. What sort of subject should you go for? Well, nature themes are always popular (cute bunny rabbits, for instance), or you can also try something symbolic (hearts, maybe), or an abstract shape (spheres or pyramids). For the uninhibited, the sky's the limit!

Trick 17: fake it!

There comes a time when even the hardiest of plants no longer thrives. For example, when deep shade, biting winds, and thick automobile pollution coincide. You can still have greenery, though — maybe with evergreen urban plants like the cherry laurel — but you'll still be lacking color and blooms.

It might not be true-to-nature, but it helps nevertheless. You can buy fake plants made of silk, wood, aluminum, or plastic. They look effective at once, and never need watering!

For laid-back gardeners

Elder, the plant with everything

It is a miracle it doesn't yet have its own fan club!

The common black elder (*Sambucus nigra*) will do its very best even with the minimum of help from the gardener. It grows just as well in shady places as in sunny ones, needs no fertilizer, can be clipped at any time, and withstands even the coldest winter without a hint of a problem. In early summer, it bears luxuriant white umbelliferous flowers from which you can make sparkling elderflower wine and little elderflower cookies. And in fall, it produces the elderberries, purplish-black fruits that can be made into delicious jellies, juices, and preserves.

Ivy

A fairytale climber that doesn't mind fumes

What it is:
- an evergreen climbing plant
- grows up to 75 feet high and 60 feet across
- normally hardy in winter (zone 5)

What it needs:
- a light-to-shady location
- regular watering in the growing season...
- ...but no build-up of water at the roots

Scientific name:
Hedera helix

The city gardener's miracle-weapon for those dark or traffic-blighted corners, ivy isn't bothered by anything much. It grows everywhere, and when it has got its teeth into something it doesn't let go. It is exhaust-resistant and will gladly entwine itself along the whole street, winding around trees and forming a reception committee at doorways and gateways.

While still young, ivy needs a climbing support, but later it develops suckers that enable it to cling to walls, trees, and fences. Only older plants flower (in the fall) but the flowers are very attractive to bees. They develop into black berries to which birds flock. Ivy is also a favorite nesting place for birds.

Buy ivy ready to plant — you should be able to find a plant that has already grown 3–4 feet in height. It does not mind whether the location is sunny or shady. It needs fertilizer every two to four weeks in the growing season. As a patio plant, it will fare best if repotted every three to four years. In the garden, ivy will act quite tame for the first few years, but after that it must regularly be cut back ruthlessly (at any time from spring through fall) or it will overrun the outside of the house and black out your windows!

You can propagate ivy in summer using leaf or stem cuttings (pages 20–21).

The plant doctor's warning: ivy berries are extremely poisonous!

Plectranthus

Unconventional

What it is:
- a small shrub grown as an annual (zone 10)
- low-growing and drooping
- a plant with attractive foliage that can put out runners of up to 7 feet in length
- insignificant white flowers in late summer or early fall

What it needs:
- full sun to partial shade
- moderate watering
- fertilizer every 14 days from March through August

Scientific name:
Plectranthus coleoides 'Marginatus', also known as Swedish Ivy, Swedish begonia, or spur flower.

Plectranthus has a heady fragrance. When you brush against its leaves, the plant gives off a camphor-like odor that is reminiscent of incense. The moths find this quite repulsive, so you won't find gypsy moths building their web-like veils in it. Yet its most notable characteristic is its ability to keep on spreading all over the place. Nothing gets in its way — walls, other plants — it grows rapidly, persistently, and is unstoppable except if pruned.

Buy plectranthus plants when they're young and plant them in the window box in May at

8–12 inch intervals. Prune now and again so that the plants grow nice and bushy. Otherwise, position them in sunshine or semishade, water them moderately during the growing season, and feed them with fertilizer once every 2 weeks. That's it!

The inconspicuous flowers appear in August or September. Plectranthus is not hardy, but if you want to keep them for longer, however, keep them indoors in winter in a light but not-too-warm location.

You can propagate plectranthus by taking cuttings (pages 20–21).

The plant doctor is satisfied that there's no chance of pests and diseases attacking plectranthus.

Aucuba

Exhaust fumes are nothing to this plant

What it is:
- a bushy evergreen shrub
- capable of reaching 5 feet in height
- notable for its dense, mostly gold-flecked or spotted foliage...
- ...and its insignificant, mostly reddish blooms early in the year...
- ...and its shiny red berries in the autumn
- capable of withstanding some frost, although not fully hardy (zone 7)

What it needs:
- partial to full shade
- protection from wind and rain
- feeding every 2 weeks in summer
- moderate watering — never let it dry out
- light, frost-free winter quarters in colder zones

Scientific name:
Aucuba japonica
Variety Tips: 'Crotonifolia', 'Picturata', and 'Variegata' are attractively flecked or spotted with colorful leaves.

You don't have to live right next to a freeway on-ramp; there are plenty of exhaust fumes

all over town — and this is when aucuba comes into its own, as the savior of the patio and city backyard, terrace, or balcony. It is certainly no rose. The blooms are hardly impressive, though the gleaming red berries are much more striking. In compensation, however, it stays green all year round and there are several variegated varieties.

This modest shrub can reach a good height (up to 5 feet), does best in shade or semi-shade, and likes to be protected from rain. It requires regular though moderate watering. Feed it regularly throughout the growing season.

If you bring aucuba indoors, keep it in a light and cool location and make sure it doesn't get too warm or dark, or it will repay you by producing dark spots on its leaves. Water it very infrequently during this period, if at all.

The plant doctor's warning: the berries are slightly poisonous.

Ice plant

Hydrophobic! Ideal for lazy people who forget to water their plants

What it is:
- a summer-flowering annual
- a low-growing plant, only 6 inches high
- yellow, orange, pink, and red to violet flowers
- flowers only open in sunlight...
- ...from late June through September

What it needs:
- a warm sunny location
- moderate watering

Scientific name:
Mesembryanthemum criniflorum or *Dorotheanthus bellidiformis*
Also known as ice plant, icicle plant, pebble plant, and fig marigold.

The ice plant flowers from July through September and comes in white, yellow, orange, pink, red, and purple varieties. The flowers resemble brightly colored marguerites, though they have shiny petals. The ice plant, as a native of South Africa, is pollution resistant but heat-loving. It grows wild in coastal California and is planted beside the freeways.

You can raise the plants yourself from seeds sown in March/April (in standard compost with a generous helping of sand mixed in). Then from mid-May onward, you can plant the seedlings out in a window box at 4-inch intervals. Or sow the seeds directly into the window box in early May. Or simply buy them ready-grown.

The ice plant has to be in the right place to do well. It likes strong sunlight — the hotter, the better. Its brilliant blooms only open fully in full sunlight and it hates the rain and having waterlogged roots. Therefore, it does best under the shelter of eaves where there is no risk of heavy rain. Water it occasionally and deadhead faded blooms.

Plant doctor's warning: waterlogged roots or heavy rain may cause fungal infection.

Berberis

A real tough cookie!

What it is:
- evergreen shrub with shallow roots
- grows 16 inches to 7 feet in height, depending on variety
- available with green or dark red leaves
- suitable for bonsai culture
- hardy in many areas (zones 4–8)

What it needs:
- sunshine to partial shade
- moderate watering in summer
- fertilizer every four weeks until August

Scientific name:
Berberis

Berberis is easy to grow and normally evergreen; it loves shade and makes a useful hedge.

Of the many varieties, plenty are suitable. One that is recommended is *Berberis buxifolia* 'Nana', a dense bushy evergreen cushion with orange-yellow flowers that grows to 16–24 inches in height. Then there is *Berberis candidula*, a semi-spherical, spreading evergreen pad of a plant with golden-yellow, slightly drooping flowers that also thrives in shady locations, but be careful of the sharp thorns! Or you could choose *Berberis thunbergii* 'Atropurpurea Nana', a dwarf upright, spreading hedge with yellowish flowers that reaches 12–24 inches and has purple-brown leaves that turn fiery red in the fall. All three varieties have shallow roots and are therefore suitable for planters, and they have bright red berries in the fall.

The berberis is an uncomplicated plant. It can stand full sun but prefers shade or semi-shade. It isn't fussy about soil type, either. During the summer growing season it needs moderate watering and feeding every 4 weeks until August. Prune it from spring through fall.

The plant doctor warns that the berries are slightly poisonous.

Alyssum

Grows, flowers, and flourishes forever

What it is:
- a low-growing, summer-flowering annual
- fast-growing and flowering
- about 4–6 inches in height
- white, pink, or lilac flower clusters ...
- ...from May through September, depending on when it was sown

What it needs:
- a sunny to semishaded location
- moderate watering
- to be cut back after the first flowering
- one application of fertilizer

Scientific name:
Alyssum maritimum or *Lobularia maritima*, also known as sweet alyssum.
Variety tips: 'Snow Carpet' and 'Snow Crystals' (both white of course!); 'Rosie O'Day' (pink); 'King's Carpet' and 'Violet Queen' (both deep purple).

This life-loving plant grows, flowers, and keeps on going — with or without help — outside in the open (on rockeries or as a quick-growing border for a flower bed) or in patio planters (even those with far too little soil). It forms dense, low-growing, white, pink, or lilac flower cushions and has a pleasant honey scent. It grows well, looks great in any kind of pot, and is ideal for filling empty spaces.

Buy alyssum ready to plant or grow it yourself (sow it 5 seeds to a pot in March/April). Plant out the seedlings at 6-inch intervals and it will flower only ten weeks later!

After a pruning with secateurs, alyssum will produce a second set of flowers, and if you have planted specimens out in stages it will bloom for the whole summer. Sometimes alyssum even does the gardener's work and seeds itself. It likes sunshine to semishade, moderate watering, and one application of fertilizer after pruning.

Catmint

Frost, drought, pollution...it can take it!

What it is:
- a herbaceous perennial
- resistant to almost anything
- adored by cats
- some varieties grow to 16–24 inches in height
- blooms pinkish-white, spotted with blue to purple
- ...from May through September
- strongly mint-scented
- fully hardy (zone 3)

What it needs:
- full sun
- little watering
- a little feeding
- shoots to be cut back after flowering

Scientific name:
Nepeta

Catmint will survive ANYTHING (frost, drought, traffic pollution) and is fully hardy. It makes no demands except for sunlight, comes up every year, and turns itself into a sea of pink or mauve blossoms from May through September. It looks good in the garden but also does well in pots. It banishes stress, odors, and the memory of rush-hour traffic, and it provides a glimpse of a rural idyll.

Buy catmint early in the year and plant it in a sunny location. The plants form loose-packed cushions with long spikes of flower heads several inches high. They are pinkish-white in the *Nepeta cataria* variety and range from lavender to purple-blue in other varieties. Catmint should be fed and watered sparingly and cut back after flowering so that it grows back thicker and puts out a second wave of blooms.

Propagate catmint by taking cuttings in spring (pages 20–21).

Honeysuckle

A tough guy!

What it is:
- a perennial climber
- this tall creeper can climb to 7–13 feet, depending on variety
- covered with clusters of yellowish-white, rose-pink, or orange-yellow tubular flowers
- ...from May through October, depending on the variety
- wonderfully scented, especially in the evening
- red or blue-black berries in the fall
- many varieties fully hardy (zones 3–7)

What it needs:
- sunshine to semishade
- plenty of water in the growing season
- never to be allowed to dry out — it actually likes having "wet feet"
- a climbing support
- pruning

Scientific name:
Lonicera

Plant care? It doesn't need any. Any other sensitivities? No, siree! Honeysuckle mingles awesome toughness (it has survived in my garden for three years in the pot in which it came, with no fertilizer or mulch) with lovely flowers and an urge to climb. It will use any support it can find, such as fences, pergolas, and balcony railings. If you want it to grow in a specific direction you will need to use wire or train it up an espalier.

Buy your honeysuckle ready to grow and plant it in a sunny position, though semi-shade will do. It needs a lot of watering when flowering — the roots must not be allowed to dry out. A handy hint for the super-lazy gardener is to plant ivy below it so that the honeysuckle's roots will be shaded. In return, you will get wonderful funnel-shaped flowers and a delightful scent, especially in the evening.

Variety tip: *Lonicera brownii* 'Dropmore Scarlet' has orange-red flowers; *Lonicera caprifolium* has yellowish or reddish blooms, a particularly strong scent, and grows to 10 feet in height; *Lonicera periclymenum* is covered in yellow-red flowers and grows to 16 feet; and *Lonicera henryi* is an evergreen variety that is especially pretty with its fragrant yellow-red blooms.

After flowering, honeysuckle should be thinned out and older, flowerless sprigs cut back. You get a bonus in fall when the plants produce berries.

In cold zones, cover the plants with straw matting or, if in a container, with sacking.

The plant doctor's warning: the berries are poisonous!

Virginia creeper

The fiery red climber

What it is:
- a deciduous vine
- an indefatigable climber, both upward and outward
- characterized by its palmate leaves...
- ...and its inconspicuous but fragrant greenish-white blooms from June to July...
- ...and its tiny blue-black berries in the fall
- hardy if properly looked after (zone 4)

What it needs:
- a sunny to semishaded position
- standard compost or loamy garden soil with humus
- support at the beginning
- generous watering in the growing season
- fertilizer every 8 weeks until August

Scientific name:
Parthenocissus quinquefolia

Virginia creeper happily displays its longevity and survival skills in Europe on the walls of old churches and castles. Anyone who longs for Sleeping-Beauty-style romanticism or the aura of the stately home ought to get a Virginia creeper.

Buy it ready to plant. Virginia creeper makes few demands. Put it in a sunny or semi-shaded position in garden soil that is not too dry, count to three, and watch it grow. In the garden it can reach 20 feet in height, depending on the variety; in a container it will naturally be more restricted. At first the new shoots will need to be tied in but later it will develop its own suckers.

Virginia creeper needs generous watering and feeding every 8 weeks until August. In the summer it can only manage to produce modest greenish-white blooms. It has a homecoming party in the fall, when the leaves turn fiery red.

Propagate Virginia creeper by taking cuttings (pages 20–21).

Silver lace vine

Car-friendly, nothing slows it down

What it is:
• a woody vine
• capable of growing 50 feet high and 40 feet wide
• characterized by its panicles of white blooms
• flowers from July through September
• fully hardy (zone 4)

What it needs:
• a sunny or semishaded location
• damp soil
• generous watering in dry conditions
• a climbing frame
• and that's all there is to it!

Scientific name:
Fallopia bald schuanica or *Polygonum aubertii*

"Tough" is this plant's middle name, "Steeplejack" is its nickname.

This is the strongest and wildest of the vines and it can easily grow by up to 20 feet in a single year. Many owners of sidewalk cafés who have tried in vain to counter the effects of traffic fumes with puny greenery eventually resort to silver lace vine. With its clouds of white flowers blooming from July through September and its luxuriant foliage, it does a brilliant cover-up job on anything in need of a disguise.

It's best to buy a container specimen of silver lace vine, as it will take too long to grow from seed. (In any case, if you go for this vine, you must be impatient by nature!) This climber is totally hassle-free. It can take sunshine, semishade, dry or damp soil —whatever you throw at it. It needs plenty of water during a dry spell, and as it doesn't have a firm grip, some kind of climbing frame is necessary.

The vine can grow to a height of several feet in a pot, but in the garden it will rapidly grow taller than a person. Suddenly you realize that drastic pruning is in order, because you can't open the window anymore! If you don't feel like spending every weekend chasing its three-foot-long tendrils with the shears, try something else. The stems soon turn thick and woody, yet in spite of everything, it is a beautiful plant.

Silver lace vine loses all its leaves in winter.

Boxwood

It really can take anything

What it is:
- an evergreen shrub
- neither pollution, wind, nor bad weather affects it
- grows to a height of 12 inches to 20 feet, depending on the variety
- known for its firm, oval, pale-to-dark green leaves and tiny yellow-green flowers
- suitable for trimming into all sorts of creative shapes...
- ...and for a career as a bonsai tree
- hardy (zones 4–5)

What it needs:
- sun or shade
- moderate watering
- monthly feeding until August
- pruning in May and August

Scientific name:
Buxus sempervirens
Variety Tip: 'Suffruticosa', a dwarf version that grows to 3 feet.

Boxwood is a pretty tough cookie. Wind, cold, wet, exhaust fumes, and industrial pollution are of no consequence. That's why it's a fairly common sight beside freeways and parkways, in urban flower beds, and on roof terraces and balconies overlooking busy traffic routes. Sometimes it's a single specimen, sometimes in groups; sometimes it's a hedge and sometimes an edge; here in the sun, there in the shade.

With its firm little evergreen leaves boxwood is not without its charms, and besides, it is very flexible. If you like it looking natural you can leave it to grow bushy, but if you prefer a more creative effect and aren't bothered about producing kitsch, you can cut it to shape — spherical, cylindrical or spiral, into a mushroom, rabbit, or swan shape. Box topiary is an old tradition in England.

Box doesn't mind whether it is in the sun or the shade. If it is to go into a container, ensure there is enough room for the roots. In a container it will obviously not grow as big, but in a garden or yard it can attain gigantic proportions.

Boxwood is happiest if kept fairly moist during the growing season, but it won't collapse if you forget to water it once in a while (which can happen). Container-grown boxwood shrubs should be fed once a month from May to August. Young plants respond to pruning in early summer by growing really thick. It's best to leave the final styling into a radical shape until the plant is about 3 or 4 years old. After this, it will need regular trimming to keep it looking neat.

The plant doctor warns that boxwood leaves are poisonous.

Phormium

If this is too hard for you, then you really are a wimp!

What it is:
- an evergreen perennial
- grows from 20 inches to 15 feet high
- not hardy (zone 8)

What it needs:
- sunshine to full shade
- plenty of water but no standing water at the roots
- a place indoors in colder zones

Scientific name:
Phormium tenax
(also known as New Zealand Flax)

With its sword-shaped leaves, phormium doesn't look fragile, and it can take a lot. Is it too dry, too wet, too sunny or too shady this summer? Whatever. Is it too dark this winter? Don't worry, be happy. Its favorite condition, however, is wet and sunny in summer, with regular feeding every two weeks. In warm summers it turns red.

Propagate phormium early in the year by division (pages 20/21).

The plant doctor warns that phormium suffers from scale insect infestation.

Shield fern

For north-facing, shady gardens only

What it is:
- elegant fern
- 12–16 inches high
- hardy in some areas (zones 4–7)

What it needs:
- shade
- moist but well-drained humus-rich soil
- watering during prolonged dry periods
- mulching from fall onward in colder zones

Scientific name:
Polystichum setiferum or *Dryopteris* spp.

These plants have been eking out a shadowy existence for over 150 million years. The hardy outdoor fern, dinosaur of the plant world, has proved that its survival qualities range from longevity to tenacity. Now it must take its chances on my north-north-west-facing balcony, and its chances are good because, as a forest plant, the fern loves shade. Its sweeping fronds give a secretive, prehistoric air to the third floor. If it is to thrive, one has to attempt to recreate the forest atmosphere, which means a location with damp soil and protection from the wind (in the garden, pep it up with leaf compost or bark mulch). During prolonged dry spells in summer the shield fern will need watering and spraying every now and then. To prepare your ferns for the winter, protect them with a layer of mulch made from leaves or wood chippings.

Ferns can be propagated by division (pages 20–21).

Periwinkle

A floral carpet – for always and everywhere

What it is:
- a dwarf evergreen shrub
- a strong-growing ground-cover plant
- 4–12 inches high
- characterized by its rich green, leathery leaves on long, rampant stems...
- ...and its extremely pretty blue, violet, red, or white blooms from April through June
- zones 4–7

What it needs:
- partial shade to shade
- damp, loamy soil
- fertilizer in the fall

Scientific name:
Vinca major (greater periwinkle) or *Vinca minor* (lesser periwinkle)

Variety tip: *Vinca major* 'Variegata', with white leaf margins and shiny blue flowers, reaching 12 inches in height; *Vinca minor* 'Rubra', with reddish-purple flowers and *Vinca minor* 'Alba' with white flowers — both 4 inches high.

Even total plant-care ignoramuses with shady plots enjoy light and color and looking for something decorative for the garden. When the lesser or greater periwinkle announces its presence, get to work fast! Periwinkle spreads a thick, soft carpet over everything capable of being covered. And during its flowering period, from April through June, it glitters with glints of blue, white, or red. It can also form an alternative lawn, because grass needs a lot more attention and doesn't look attractive during all seasons of the year.

Sounds great — so far. But is there no shady side to this shady plant? Actually, there is, because periwinkle is quite merciless toward weaker plants, so anything that cannot withstand it gets smothered. So plant it in moderation and always keep it under control.

Buy periwinkle seedlings and plant at 12-inch intervals in loamy soil. The runners will soon take root and multiply. Planting times are early in the year or in the fall. Apply fertilizer in the fall.

Swan River daisy

An iron hand in a velvet glove

What it is:
• a summer-flowering annual with a bushy growth pattern
• like a blue daisy in appearance...
• ...with thin, pinnate leaves
• 8–18 inches high
• flowers from May through September...
• ...in white, pink, blue, or purple varieties
• easy to tend and robust

What it needs:
• full sun
• enough room to send out tendrils
• regular watering but no waterlogged roots
• fertilizing every week or two

Scientific name:
Brachycome iberidifolia

In its native Australia the Swan River daisy grows between stones and in cracks in the rock — good training that has helped this little blue flower to become pretty tough and hardy. And it needs to be tough if it's to have any joy at all on our hot, south-facing balcony next to a six-lane highway.

The most striking feature of the Swan River daisy is its incredibly fast growth. In its first summer with us, it has grown as if it were being paid to do so, and flowered as if it were trying to win a flower show medal. From early in the year through to the fall it has been continuously studded with lots of little daisy blooms. It gets quite bushy and tends to resemble a 1970s Afro hairstyle in sky blue (though some varieties have pink or white flowers).

The Swan River daisy should be purchased ready to plant from the middle of May and planted in a sunny position at 6-inch intervals. It looks best in rock gardens, around the edges of planters on the balcony, or against a wall; then it can run wild over balustrades and fences in need of a bit of beautifying.

In return for all this, it asks for nothing more than regular watering (neither saturation nor drought) and some fertilizer every two weeks. And that's all.

You can propagate Swan River daisies by seed or cuttings (pages 18–19 and 20–21).

Erigeron (Fleabane)

Never gone with the wind!

What it is:
• a perennial flowering shrub...
• ...only at its best in the first year
• a fast-growing and luxuriant plant with many branches
• grows up to 12 inches high
• ideal for windy balconies
• in flower from May through September...
• ...first in white, then in red

What it needs:
• sunshine
• moderate watering
• fertilizer every two weeks

Scientific name:
Erigeron karvinskianus

Erigeron, too, has its origins in areas where survival is no picnic, namely in rock crevices with sparse soil and in cracks in walls in places like Mexico and Venezuela. It has evolved to withstand even strong winds, which makes it ideal for skyscraper balconies.

Erigeron grows with one burst of speed into a broad, bushy pillow. From May through

September it is dotted with miniature blooms, white at first and then tending to turn red, like the daisies that grow wild in the meadows. In addition it shows a marked inclination to trail, which is good for hanging baskets and particularly so for parapet walls and balcony balustrades.

You can grow it yourself. To do so, you must sow the seeds from January to March/April, cover them lightly with dirt, and keep them in a warm place (at room temperature, in fact). The seedlings need to be fed every 14 days and kept fairly moist. Or you can buy plants from the middle of May and plant them out at 8–12-inch intervals. Water them moderately (they don't like to get too wet), feed every 14 days, and dead-head them regularly.

There is another European plant called fleabane (*Inula dysenterica*), sometimes called blue fleabane, in order to distinguish it from this Central American variety.

The plant doctor likes fleabane, which is indeed the bane of fleas and other diseases and pests.

What to plant with it:
Flowers with a fairly wild nature make suitable companions for erigeron; for example, lavender (page 45), bellflower (*Campanula*, page 73), and sage (page 52).

Tobacco plant

It may look lacy and frilly, but it's tough

What it is:
• a bushy annual
• in flower from July through September...
• ...with white, cream, yellow, pink, or deep-red blooms
• from 12–40 inches in height
• strongly scented

What it needs:
• lots of sunshine
• lots of watering
• fertilizer once a week

Scientific name:
Nicotiana x *sanderae*

At last there's a really pleasant way to kick the habit of smoking. Just switch over to tobacco plants. Enjoyment without self-denial! Tobacco plants look very attractive in window boxes and planters, with their many lovely blooms in white, yellow, pink, or red. Despite its delicate appearance — it looks like the sort of frilly cap worn by Whistler's Mother — it is actually a very tough plant. City balconies don't bother it at all, and it takes both heat and high wind in its stride.

There are plenty of varieties to choose from, of which *Nicotiana* x *sanderae* is the most popular, though *Nicotiana alata*, *N. suaveolens,* and *N. sylvestris* are more fragrant, especially in the evening. Sensitive noses should not sniff too often — over-indulgence can bring on a headache. Perhaps it was this strong aroma that caused French envoy Jean Nicot to bring this unknown plant home on his voyage from South America and offer it as a gift to the kings of France and Portugal, more than 500 years ago. In any case, he gave it his name and a new home on our balconies.

You can buy tobacco plants from early summer or grow them yourself from seeds sown in February/March. Standard compost or container compost will do and a sunny position is advisable. The plants will form loose bushes of about 12–40 inches high if they are thriving.

No matter how robust they are, tobacco plants still require a minimum of attention. This means they should be watered regularly and fed weekly. Any wilted flowers need to be snipped off.

The plant doctor warns that the tobacco plant is poisonous from root to flower. Unfortunately, this doesn't bother snails and slugs in the least — they love munching on them. And even aphids seem to be irresistibly drawn to them.

Resources and Bibliography

Resources

www.gardennet.com
Information, shopping guide, gardening resources, discussion groups.

Abundant Life Seed Foundation
Non-profit organization promoting the conservation and use of heirloom, native and rare seeds. Information, seeds, education programs, newsletter.
PO Box 772, Port Townsend WA 98368
www.abundantlifeseed.org

Cyndi's Catalogue of Garden Catalogues
Links to over 1,900 mail order gardening catalogues in Canada and the U.S. organized by location and product.
www.qnet.com/~johnsonj/

www.eseeds.com
Seeds and supplies from mail order and online companies worldwide.

Johnny's Selected Seeds
Organic seeds, including vegetables, medicinal and culinary herbs and flowers.
www.johnnyseeds.com

Burpee
Vegetable, flower and herb seeds and accessories. One of the world's oldest and largest garden seed companies.
www.burpee.com

Gardener's Supply Company
Classic gardening supplies, tools and furniture.
128 Intervale Road, Burlington, VT 05401
www.gardeners.com

Smith and Hawken
Elegant tools and supplies.
www.smithandhawken.com
1-800-940-1170

Windowbox.com
Witty website offering supplies for container gardening.

The Intimate Gardener
Garden furniture and nifty accessories.
4215 North Sheridan Road, Chicago, IL 60613
www.theintimategardener.com

Jackson and Perkins
Prize winning roses, plus flowers and accessories.
1-800-292-4769
www.jacksonandperkins.com

American Meadows
Regional and custom wildflower mixes.
americanmeadows.com

Planet Natural
Organic seeds and earth-friendly gardening supplies and pest controls.
1612 Gold Ave., Bozeman MT 59715
1-800-289-6656
www.planetnatural.com

Books

Gardening By Mail, 5th Ed.
By Barbara Barton and Ginny Hunt
Houghton Mifflin, 1997

*The Blooming Great Gardening Book:
A Guide for All Seasons*
By Steve Whysall
Whitecap Books, 2000

Colorful Hanging Baskets and Other Containers
By Tessa Evelegh and Debbie Patterson
Whitecap Books, 2001

Index

Scientific (Botanical or Latin) plant names

142

Imprint

About the Authors

Sybille Engels
- is an editor and the owner of a publishing house
- has been working on Basic Books from the start
- doesn't know exactly which she likes best, gardening or publishing books. With both of them, there's always something new to discover and the journey never ends
- has always wanted to write a book that would combine both of her passions, and this in a Basic way
- has always wanted to write a book with Veronika Goldstück who is an old friend of hers

Veronika Goldstück
- an editor and indefatigable balcony gardener
- can hardly hold herself back when the spring arrives (absolutely crazy about buying flowers)
- loves everything wild growing as well as Alpine meadows, huge sunflowers and green guests
- inspired her friend Sybille Engels with gardening pleasure and herself with book writing

The rest of the Basic team

Martina Görlach
- mainly photographs food
- finds cherries in the neighbor's garden much less attractive than those on her own balcony
- that's why she really enjoyed taking pictures of all the plants in *Basic Gardening*
- Favorite chapter: Gourmet à la carte – so beautiful you want to eat it up!!!

Andrea Holzer
- a photographer from Italy's mountains
- with particular love for detail
- bravely defended her home-grown against lice, etc.

Ulla Krause
- a stylist and a hopeless romantic
- infatuated with flowery table arrangements
- could live her passion to the fullest
- also brought along anything a Basic Gardener might need

Roberto Simoni
- a photographer from southern Italy
- from his camera came the people shots
- admits that his only green thumb is the one that presses the shutter

Antonia Adam
- is the gourmet who did the recipe testing for this book
- and the most delightful melonseed-spitting champion in the world

Nico Becker
- is our mister turbo
- is quick at preparing food
- he loves climbing plants — yet even more, rocks with no plants to climb

Marion Schwenninger
- our Asian plant expert
- gardening isn't work for her, it is pure meditation
- loves cottage gardens and everything British

Dieter Wirthmann
- the Mediterranean type
- his gardening motto is: enjoy and let others do the watering
- needed six weeks vacation in the sun after a shoot lasting only four days

Thomas Jankovic
- Art Director and Graphic Designer
- developed the Basic Look
- was ready for the challenge and became an enthusiastic participant in the project

Birgit Hausenberger
- was a busy bee as an editor trying to get the Basic team together
- the plant that wants to survive with her must water itself or conquer her boy-friend's heart
- in spite of that she has huge success with things like amaranth, sunflowers, and grass (oh, the wonder of nature!)

Kirsten Sonntag
- is a freelance editor
- has edited many books on gardening
- but none of them so sensationally Basic as this
- apart from the work on *Basic Gardening* she was busy night and day trying to expel legions of snails from her city garden — unfortunately to no avail, but at least it worked out with the book....

Ute Hausleiter
- motivated lithographers, typesetters and printers to publish *Basic Gardening*

Acknowledgements:

Dr. Wolfgang Hensel the author of many books on gardening and supported us with a critical check of the text
Herrn Fuchsenthaler vom Gartencenter Dehner the author of many books on gardening and supported us with a critical check of the text
Maria Lucas from the Dehner Garden Center who not only supplied us with plants, flower pots and watering cans but also gave us a hand and advice at the photo shoot
Heide Kawerau for her wonderful balcony and the accessories from Schuldenberg, Germany
Gerald Schreiber who lent his dreamlike terrace where working was almost like spending a vacation
Nina Kolibius for her active support before and during the shoot
Christine and Eugen Hausenberger for their butterfly meadow, which is no more, and the caring cultivation (raising) of the plants
Rolo König for the poppy flower campaign
Sompex which provided us with gardening tools
Gärtnerei Buchner, Anneliese Müller, Munich; **Samen Schmitz**, Munich and Dornach; **Le Prince Jardinier**, France; **Intacado**, Langenfeld; **Two's Company Europe**, France as well as the Munich **Botanical Garden** for their help with photo production
And **all our colleagues and friends** for their emotional and moral support

Photo credits

Martina Görlach, Foodphotography Eising: all pictures of plants (except p.74 r., 103 l., 104 d/r., 112 r.); the 14 Basic Elements (except p.10 center above) and the Green 17; Special Party, Styling and Water (except the pictures of people), the shots on the cover slip overleaf and the cover flower, pic.pp., 15, 18, 19, 20, 24, 27, 28, 31, 37, 43, 56, 69, r., 92, 109, 126, 127
Roberto Simoni: all pictures of people, pp., 14, 22, 36, 61 r.
Ernst Neukamp: p.10 center above
Marion Nickig: p.74 r., 103 l., 104 b r., 112 r.

German edition © Copyright 2001 Gräfe und Unzer Verlag GmbH, Munich, Germany
Editing: Birgit Hausenberger, Kirsten Sonntag
Cover design and layout: Thomas Jankovic & Sybille Engels
Layout: Ute Hausleiter
English translation: American Pie, London, UK
Typesetting: Filmsatz Schröter, München
Reproduction: Penta, München
Printing and binding: Druckhaus Kaufmann, Lahr

Printed in Germany